ENDORSEMENTS FOR

PRETTY

"Pretty is one of those books ... ...nt want to put down. It's challenging, heartbreaking, encouraging and inspiring. I love that she isn't afraid to be real with her readers about what living honestly really looks like. More importantly, I believe her when she says that striving for perfection is nothing but an empty illusion and that I was made for so much more. This book begins a much-needed conversation about what it means to really love each other and ourselves, and I can't recommend it strongly enough."

— RUTH SOUKUP
New York Times best-selling author of
Living Well Spending Less: 12 Secrets of the Good Life
and founder of LivingWellSpendingLess.com

"This book pretty much reads like the inside of my heart. Tammy's book encourages readers to look beyond the superficialities we use to protect ourselves or to impress others and to examine the illusions that prevent us from authentic connection."

— EMILY LEX
Founder of Jones Design Company
and Blogger at JonesDesignCompany.com

"Deeply insightful, and refreshingly honest, Pretty dives into the beautiful and complicated life of women. It speaks to the lies we've been dealt and how we continue to sit at the table and play that hand, even if we know better. This book is about having courage, finding inner strength, and living free. Tammy is a soulful, beautiful writer. You will be blessed by her story and by this book!"

— KRISTA GILBERT

Author of *Reclaiming Home*
and blogger at Meaning in a Minute

"I know this book was written primarily for women, but any guy with a wife or daughters needs to read this book! Tammy Strait is insightful, encouraging, and challenging in this wonderful work of grace and true beauty. I was intrigued by her transparency and blessed by her heart. I highly recommend this amazing book!"

— KURT BUBNA

Author of *Epic Grace*

PRETTY

BREAKING FREE FROM THE ILLUSIONS OF OF A SUPERFICIAL LIFE

by Tammy Strait

Fedd Books
401 Ranch Rd. 620 S.
Ste. 250
Austin, TX 78734

Editing by Cara Highsmith, Highsmith Creative Services, www.highsmithcreative.com
Cover Design by Shannon Payne
Interior Design by Blake Atwood with EditFor.me

Unless otherwise noted, all scripture quoted is from the NIV translation. New International Version (niv) –
THE HOLY BIBLE, NEW INTERNATIONAL VERSION®, NIV® Copyright © 1973, 1978, 1984, 2011 by Biblica, Inc.® Used by permission. All rights reserved worldwide.

ISBN: 978-1507697504
Printed in the United States of America

First Edition 14 13 12 11 10 / 10 9 8 7 6 5 4 3 2

Dedicated to my three future daughters-in-law:

For someday,
we will be in love with the same boy.

CONTENTS

WHY I WROTE THIS BOOK

I've never been content to be who I am. Maybe it's better or more appropriate to say I've never been comfortable staying the same. Either way, perhaps both, my life up to this point has been a journey of finding out who I am, and why I've been so afraid to be her.

The truth of my story is probably much like your own: it's been woven with heartbreak. I've wrestled with my particular suffering long enough to learn that the only way for me to make sense of it is to share it. Not necessarily to find a solution or garner some semblance of peace, though that seems to be an unexpected and very welcomed byproduct, but to confirm a very optimistic assumption that I'm not alone.

A deeply rooted suspicion I've had that when the masks are off and the walls are down we really are connected, even in our brokenness. Perhaps even, especially there. And despite the ways we try to make our lives pretty on the outside, when the unruly nature of our real selves spills over into our reality at some level we know we are not alone.

This book is my journey. You might think of it a journal, of sorts. A place where I question who I am, what I have suffered, and determine how I can use it to make me stronger. It is my hope and fervent prayer that it helps you even a tiny fraction of what it has done for me.

INTRODUCTION
Calling Out the Illusion

S ettling down into a hard folding chair I try to embrace my front row seat to the public school system. Just a kindergarten mom at her first school board meeting, I wasn't prepared for the one-two punch I was about to face. Nor was I aware that this meeting would become a turning point in my life—that it would move me to write this book.

The room fills with hushed chatter on both sides of the aisle as we wait for the meeting to begin. The entry is standing room only and the muggy September evening adds a foreboding heat to a room already thick with tension. Anticipation, disdain, fear, and uncertainty hang like a dense fog in the air. It was evident that after a long-smoldering political debate, tonight a fight was on. In the face of bitter division, hurled insults and slander, and political battle lines clearly drawn, I maintain my efforts to remain neutral. Avoiding eye contact with acquaintances on both sides of the fray I steel myself to stay objective. But my nerves and resolve are silently unraveling from the seething words of the woman behind me.

Every petition by a woman sharing her political opinion is lauded as smart, "What a sweet, charming woman." Every woman making a statement against her position is chastised. Demeaned. Audibly scorned those of us in proximity. After numerous insults my nerves get the better of me. I casually turn around and say as sweetly and calmly as I can, "You know, (ahem) you have every right to speak before the board if you have something to say."

She looks at me, her formerly glossy, self-entertained eyes glazing over in a dull, angry haze. Her Cheshire grin quickly vanishes from her lips as they slowly pull into a taut line, curling slightly at the corner in a glint of disgust. She looks at me, intently, realizing for the first time that though I sit on her side of the aisle, I'm not necessarily in line with her perspective. But more important, I don't find her snide commentary amusing. I feel the tension rising between our silent stares. As if giving me a compliment, she looks directly in my face and says, "Well," looking away for a moment to add weight to her next statement, "At least you're pretty."

I stare intently into her cool, unblinking eyes for a moment, letting her insult sink all the way in. Then, deliberately, and without any response, I turn around in my chair. My calm demeanor belies the vexing turbulence in my mind. She knows. She knows what she said, she knows what she meant, and she knows I saw through her thinly-veiled guise and took a sucker punch to the gut.

It takes strength not to hit her back. Not to walk into the trap she has laid perfectly before me—a trap to draw out my anger and unleash a tangled fury buried beneath my flesh. A torrent of wild words could flow so quickly; words I can never take back. It's the trap of the fool, one I've fallen in too many times to count. But this time I know better, and I don't want to give her the satisfaction. Not this time.

I have learned there is wisdom found in restraint. It is moments like this—when everything in you wants to fight back, raise hell, or put someone in her place—you must choose to take the high road. Digging deep within, you find the courage to withhold. Biting your tongue if you must, you choose to stay above the fray. This is not the seat of passivity or weakness, but one of wisdom and strength.

If you've taken this road, you know it takes everything you've got. How much easier would it be to lash back in anger, vengeance, or our selfish pursuit of justice? If we're honest, that is what we desire. To withhold is not our nature; it goes against everything we know about self-preservation and self-defense. And yet, it's the greatest weapon we have.

I didn't look at her the rest of the night, but her words stayed with me. They haunted me. Not because I believed what she said, or rather the insinuation behind her back-handed compliment, but because what she said captured the essence of a "mean girls" game some grown women still play: *If you're on my side we can be friends and I really don't care what you think as long as it's what I think. But if you challenge me, disagree with me, or stand up for your beliefs against me I will tear you down. I will make your life hard. I will gossip, intimidate, demean, lie; I will cut you down and slander you.*

To her, my words didn't matter. My thoughts, my feelings, my opinions, and my intelligence—everything inside of me that makes me, me—none of it mattered. To her, I was just another pretty face. She knew exactly what she was doing. Like so many other mean girls who never got a good look in the mirror, she lives her life in the punishing grip of insecurity and in fearful, irrational, and hurtful competition with other women.

It doesn't matter if you're in the corporate world or at the mommy-and-me play date, if one woman has something the others don't have or want, she immediately becomes a threat. Their lives revolve around the external; they have bought into the marketer's pitch that perception is reality, that only the packaging counts. However, behind the pretty wrapper is a product marked with pain, loss, and grief. Inside, we're all the same.

"Here pretty, pretty . . . ," like calling a kitten to milk, our culture lures girls and women of all ages into the trap of *pretty*. Being pretty, looking pretty, talking pretty, dressing pretty, while covering up our true human nature underneath—the part that isn't so pretty. We add layer upon layer of "pretty" over the judgment, jealousy, unforgiveness, competitiveness, and brokenness trapped just beneath the surface of a put-together life.

As a culture and as women, we value the external appearance and illusion of pretty. As young girls we strive to fit in with the popular crowd, those who have the right clothes, hair, makeup, and attitude to set them apart as the "pretty girls." We learn at a very young age what qualifies as pretty, what pretty does, and who pretty is . . . and what attitudes and behaviors are likely to get us thrown on our pretty little behinds.

As we grow into young women we continue to strive for pretty in so many ways. Cattiness and downright meanness develops in young peer groups; girls are left out of the group; lines are drawn as to who makes the cut. More often than not, pretty girls are seen in packs, while some truly beautiful girls are left by the wayside because of jealousy, insecurity, and competitiveness.

There's nothing pretty about it!

As adult women, we continue to value the illusion of pretty. We secretly revere those women who exude an image of having it all together: perfectly dressed in the latest designer brands, hair perfectly groomed, with the admiring, successful husband and stylishly dressed and well-behaved kids enrolled in sports, music, and all the popular activities; they throw the hippest, most fun parties and have the latest and greatest toys and gadgets. They seem to have it all—the extravagant life, happy home, thriving kids, check, check, check. Their lives appear to be perfect.

Except it's a sham! An illusion. Especially with kids, a pretty world and pretty life just doesn't exist. This "pretty" that we valiantly strive and sacrifice for, covet and would die for isn't real. On some level every single one of us knows it, and yet we still seek to achieve it; make it our own. We fool ourselves into believing that we've got it together; we carry on the lie, expending precious time and energy trying to convince those around us that we actually have this thing—this elusive perfect life—but it's a game, an exhausting empty game of charades that leaves us grasping at the wind, living a seemingly endless lie.

We were made for more than pretty. We were made for grace.

Within each of us resides a story of a broken life: a dream, a childhood, a painful mistake, or failed relationship. Behind our fragile flesh are the enduring scars of brokenness. There is not one who escapes the harsh reality of this life. Not one. It is only by being truthful with ourselves and others that we find healing for our wounds. It comes in risking the façade, being vulnerable, exposing our flawed authentic selves to the healing light of truth with safe, grace-filled and loving people.

In deep, authentic community we discover we are not alone in our struggling or our suffering. Each of us walks painful roads of rejection, abandonment, abuse, jealousy, addiction, and grief. Exploring the cavernous depths of our broken lives we discover our true self and find love and acceptance, compassion and grace.

Only through the lens of our shared brokenness do we see that we are better together—a tapestry woven of the finest fabric of the human experience and the enduring faithfulness of a Heavenly Father who offers us wholeness.

I wish I could tell you that looking back on my life that all the painful stories make sense. I want to say that the memory of them stops hurting, but that wouldn't be entirely true. I wish I could promise you that the story changes. But it won't. What I can say is that all the painful rejections, exclusions, and abandonments by some of the people I loved the most were not in vain. Every heartache carved out something in me that is deep and real and more beautiful than was ever there before. No matter that we may never understand why we've been hurt, it is up to us to find the purpose for the pain.

The threads of family run deep. The tapestry of our lives is very much told in the story of family. Broken, mended, patched, or threadbare—each of us holds a story carved on the walls of our hearts, and we carry the burdens on our backs. Family. Our parents. Grandparents. Our siblings. The friends we have chosen, the community in which we live. The people we choose to have in our lives shape our experience.

But, how can we love well in a world of broken, hurting people who hurt other people? How do we live fully and well in a world full to the brim with pain? How do we live deeper than a superficial pretty life? How might we allow the many trials to carve character and lead us to true beauty, found in the depths of self-acceptance and authenticity?

The answer: We find our courage.

Because we're going to need it.

We find our strength hidden in the deepest places of our spirit and we build. We choose to build hope, truth. We choose to build encouragement, love, and grace. We decide to take that first brave step into an authentic life, speaking the truth about our lives, our stories, our joy and our pain: all of us. We step into the life that we have, and not the life that we wish we had.

In that moment, the revolution of hope can begin. Then we throw off what weighs us down and boldly design an unhindered life. But first we've got to be real. It's the birthplace of freedom.

I will tell you very honestly, I cannot find an easy answer or a miraculous truth that sets us free. Believe me, I've tried all the easy ways. We live in a broken world, and the reality is that it is getting darker and meaner every day. And so we must choose to build. You and I.

Each day, each moment we have to choose: Will we build our homes? Will we build our lives, our marriages, our children, our communities, our relationships and extended family, our SELVES? Or will we tear it all down with our very own hands by bitter words and hurtful actions?

So in the midst of pain and brokenness we must seek after and find truth. Truth requires us to step outside of and die to ourselves—die to the reactor, the aggressor, the justifier, and the defender in each of us. We must strip away the layers we've built to protect our hearts and stop throwing arrows when there is no war. There is no greater challenge than to die to self and restrain our human nature. We choose to take the sucker punch of this broken, weary life, and continue to do the right thing. We continue to love, not because we feel it, but because it's our greatest command.

Truth often goes against our strongest of feelings; it cuts against the raging feelings of injustice, anger, and revenge. Truth interferes with our selfish desire to be right. But when you can *look back* on your life, your family, and the journey you've traveled with a new vision; *look in* to your self and find the extraordinary beauty that resides in the broken, while you *look out* for the predictable thorns that get in the way, you will begin to *look forward* to the life you were intended to live, and you will *look up* and find a Father who works all things for your good. And then, you will see that the story never changed. But you did.

You see; it was never about the story. It was about you.

This is not a book for those seeking an easy journey. I offer no trite explanations or blanket solutions to the ever-changing complexities of emotion and experience that underlie human relationships. It is not a channel through which I espouse platitudes or pretend I have things figured out. I know all too well my own personal failures and weaknesses and how far I fall short and how often I succumb to my selfish nature.

This book is about starting a dialogue with ourselves and other women, being open, honest, and vulnerable, creating a safe place to call out the illusion of a pretty life whereby we can boldly venture into the deep hidden places of our souls and find healing. Find what is real.

Together we're going to take a look on the inside. We're going to unmask brokenness and reveal the character traits that we attempt to push down into the darkness where we think no one can see. We're going to stop trying to hide the torn flesh and patchwork scars hidden beneath the surface of our superficial lives. We're going to spend some time and energy on our hearts, minds, and spirits, making the imperative investment in our souls.

Pretty won't begin to capture the beauty. Aligned on our inside, our external will fall woefully short of the beauty of our hearts and spirits. We've got to be full of something other than ourselves: Pretty doesn't cut it anymore.

PART ONE
LOOKING BACK

1: PRETTY PRINCESS
The Rise and Fall of a Dream

I am a princess not because I have a prince.
But because my Father is a King and He is God.
~Author Unknown

I was raised in a quaint little town in northern Wisconsin. A root beer colored river meandered through its center and I grew up on its bank. We had one small high school, fifteen bars, and about the same number of churches. A single flashing red light marked the intersection of the four corners of a little city where everyone knew your name. My parents owned a restaurant and my dad was once the mayor, so people I didn't know knew my name.

Growing up I found it annoying and small. It's funny how we never fully appreciate the gifts we are given in the moment—always seeking after and longing for something more, something different from what we have. I thought my life painfully simple. For a young girl that means boring. Had I wanted to run wild, I would've inevitably been caught, and quickly. As it was, I lived a pretty uneventful childhood. With a defiant older brother and a reckless younger sister I had plenty of second-hand experiences to glean from. As God would have it, second-hand learning seemed to satisfy my curiosity, and still does.

I look back now on the roots that began to grow in a small town and am thankful. The older I get, the more I'm drawn back to those childhood roots and the things that remind me of a simpler life. In many ways, it was a much more meaningful time. People talked on the phone. If I wanted to play with a friend I had to call them and actually talk to them! It was an accomplishment to memorize and know my friend's phone numbers by heart. When we were together we focused on each other. Without the distractions of today, relationships were about *relationship*. In more ways than one, we knew each other by heart.

Some of my most favorite memories growing up include two particular childhood friends. Our days consisted of swimming in that root beer river and diving for rings at the bottom of a pool all summer long. We snuggled up under one of my grandma's handmade quilts, took turns buttering saltine crackers, and played waitress. We rode our bikes up the bridge to the A&W to drink root beer frosties and devour baskets of salty french fries, or we would go to the auto-stop to buy Mr. Freeze pops. Sometimes we'd do both in one day. We played for hours in a backyard dollhouse and set up lemonade stands on the street.

We played neighborhood games until late in the night with the kids on our street. The big tree in our front yard was "ghoul." We dressed all in black with paint on our faces to camouflage us in the dark. As we would scatter to hide in the black of night and try to make our way back to ghoul without being caught, we never once considered we weren't safe. We were free to explore. We learned to be street smart but we were never unsafe. This was a community of kids who looked after each other; we learned how to play and have fun.

This was the life of a small town: simple and sheltered, and yet so very sweet. As a mom now, I think back to the memories of my childhood and wish I could provide the same experiences for my children. But we live in a different time. No longer are children free to ride their bikes into town by themselves with change in their pockets for treats at the local malt shop. Nor are they safe to play neighborhood games late into the night with no supervision.

As life becomes more technologically "connected" and complex, we're losing our innocence. Children are forced to grow up faster, and notions of play no longer hold the same meaning and power of connection and community. Relationships are more about status or numbers than quality time with people. With instant access to unlimited Internet, kids are prey for acts of violence in the safety of their own homes. We are slowly losing the magic of childhood.

THE FAIRYTALE PRINCESS

When I was a little girl I loved all the Disney princess movies. I can't say I remember dressing up like a princess, maybe I did, but I certainly loved watching them—how they moved, how they lived so fully and unapologetically in their own skin. I was fascinated by their deepest thoughts, what they loved, how they danced and twirled and sang their way through life. In my childlike eyes, it was the image of what it was to be a woman. Beauty personified.

What a set up. What a tragic fairytale for the rest of us girls, right? Maybe not.

We have heard a lot about the negative messages contained in these fairytales; but, looking back on some of my favorite childhood princesses, I believe we are only remembering a part of who they were. Captured or distracted by her amazing beauty, most of us have forgotten the far more beautiful things about the girls in these stories.

Belle was fiercely smart. She educated herself and dared to follow the ambitions of her own mind, despite her critics. She stood for her principles and was never afraid to say no. She was brave, willing to sacrifice herself and her happiness for the life and freedom of her father.

Ariel was determined to find her own way in the world. She faced her life and her dreams head on. Taking risks and challenging authority that set rules without grace, she was independent, curious, industrious, brave, and kind. She dared to dream and follow those dreams whatever the cost.

Cinderella, a delicate girl with a beautiful face, had a grown-up heart overflowing with love. Blessed with a servant's heart, she was honest, unassuming, compassionate, and kind. Unafraid of her own voice she found happiness in the quiet confines of her conscripted world and exemplified a timeless grace.

Nothing but a pretty face? I say not.

As children, not only did we see those things, we were drawn to those things. Because as much as there was an obvious external beauty, there was an inner radiance—a beauty that extended far beyond the confines of her flesh and went as deep as her soul. Each held a timeless elegance composed of kindness, compassion, strength, and grace.

As children, we are not distracted by external packaging. It takes years of social conditioning before children recognize what seem like obvious differences to adults. Children look with eyes that see past the exterior to a real and compassionate heart. As children, we saw and were drawn to the true heart of a princess.

But looking back, so many of us neglect to see the characteristics that made her truly beautiful. We've defined her only by a pretty face. We've made the princess and her heart the brunt of our bitter or sarcastic jokes because we've forgotten *who* she is. And in so doing, we've forgotten *who* we are.

As adults we've lost the ability to see with the eyes of a child—the ability to look past the exterior and see the content of a persons character. We think notions of princesses are passé at best and most certainly frivolous, so we encourage our daughters to hurry through this stage for fear it will ruin them completely. But we've forgotten that a princess is more than a pretty package. It's a condition of the heart.

PROGRESSIVE PRINCESS

For generations of women who grew up with the image and heart of a princess, the women's movement changed everything.

Bolstered by rightful outrage for women's rights, the momentum of a movement carried a tidal wave of repercussions far beyond what these brave women envisioned. I have no intention of adding to the divide over the women's movement because it brought so many important issues to the forefront and changed the face of what it means to be a woman in our time. I have the right to vote. I had the freedom to go to law school and the liberty to pursue any dream I wished. These are the gifts of a movement.

But in giving women unlimited opportunities it had, perhaps, the unintended effect of shutting others down. Women who longed to remain in the home to raise their families were seen as weak, antiquated, and somehow secondary to those women choosing this newer, more progressive path.

The princesses we loved as a girl lost the beauty so intrinsically tied to being a woman, and became seen as weak, pathetic, helpless beauty queens who only needed to be saved. We stopped looking at the traits that made these women female—all of which made them beautiful—and focused only on their pretty little faces.

Women were encouraged to harden a once soft heart and begin to fit into a new mold. The movement pushed women to power, and in the crush of the tidal wave, some women began to take on not only masculine roles, but also masculine character traits. Strength increasingly became confused with aggression. At the expense of our femininity, we're losing the battle to empower women and losing the true heart of a woman.

I posed a question on my blog asking my readers which were their favorite childhood princess and why. The very first response bluntly attacked these princesses as helpless beauties that always needed to be rescued. I was feeling disappointed that this was the first response to the question, and that it had pretty much shut down any further discussion, when my husband blessed me with the true heart of a man.

He asked me, "Do you want to know my favorite princess?" I looked at him halfway and rolled my eyes thinking, *Yeah, right, this will help.* Uninvited, he continued: "My favorite was Princess Leia because though she never needed someone to rescue her, she let him anyway."

In one sentence my husband recaptured my heart and communicated what I've known but couldn't articulate: The true heart of a man desires to rescue his love, and the truest heart of a woman *wants* him to.

We were made by God to be together—and the two will become one flesh. We are helpers to one another in fellowship, friendship, and deep abiding intimacy. We are to be strength when one is weak, to rescue one another from harm, and to save us from ourselves.

In a culture so motivated by progressivism and rife with cruel judgment, we've become jaded about what our roles are, and we're losing the femininity that was created in us. This is not to say women can't or shouldn't be in powerful leadership roles. Not by a long shot. But, the most successful women leaders continue to embody that which makes them feminine. In fact, I believe women can be even more successful, leading with the subdued strength that intrinsically makes them a woman. Women have far more power harnessing the strength that lies in the beauty and grace of their femininity than assuming the demeanor of a man. Some of the most powerful women today do just that. We were made, not to be pretty, but to embody all the characteristics of a princess.

> The fruit of the spirit is love, joy, peace, forbearance, kindness, goodness, faithfulness, gentleness and self-control. Against such things there is no law.
> — Galatians 5:22-23

You see, a princess is not just pretty on the outside; she is beautiful on the inside where it counts. Think back on your favorite fairytale princess and you will see the fruit of the spirit in her life. And you will see her allow a man to love her with a man's heart—she lets him rescue her despite the fact that she could surely save herself because she loves him.

MORE THAN A PRINCESS

Growing up I remember many times being ridiculed and called a "princess." My mom and sister have been known to characterize me that way. Even one of my teachers in high school got angry with me when I stood up to her for something she was doing that was unjust. In anger, she lashed out at me, saying that I was being a princess. Let's just say she didn't mean it as a compliment. I'm sure there are many others who've called me a princess as an insult.

In my last year of college I met a young woman who played on a rugby team. She was my opposite in nearly every way, but I believe she respected me as much as I respected her. As tender as I was, she was rough. As mild as I was, she was wild. I was training for my first marathon and despite our differences she knew I was working hard to make a new life and overcome some pretty big setbacks.

She worked at a local screen-printing shop and one day she came to our house with a sweatshirt she made for me. It was similar to the one she had made for her entire rugby team. Across the back was the number she assigned me: 26.2 for the miles of a marathon. On the front should have been my name. But she chose nicknames for her teammates, and arched across the entire front of the sweatshirt was the name she had chosen for me. In big, bold, black capital letters, it read: PRINCESS.

At the time I wasn't sure if she was making fun of me. I still wear it from time to time and think of her, but I didn't give the nickname much thought until now. Despite how different we were and the different the lives we had lived, there was a soft part of her that I know loved my soft princess heart. Just as there was a tough part of me that loved her strong, resilient spirit.

It makes me sad so many women have not only forgotten what they knew to be so true as a child, they've become hostile to it. We've abandoned the notion of being a princess because we're afraid to stand against the current of our culture. Or we've completely forgotten the eternal beauty of a princess's heart. It was never about her pretty face to me. I didn't know it at the time, but I longed for the beauty of *who* she was.

But just as so many didn't see the depth beneath the surface, I failed see the struggle so deeply imbedded in her life. Most fairytales have a daring prince rescuing his princess; I'll give you that. However, it's the superficial storyline. As I look back into the stories of the princesses I watched as a little girl, not only did their inner beauty captivate the attention of the princes (and the audience), it incited hatred from the women in their paths—the many critics who blatantly called out for her fall.

Far too often we live on the surface of life. We see the fairytale princess and delude ourselves into thinking she has suffered nothing. After all, she has a beautiful body and a pretty face, what suffering could there be? We believe that if it all looks good on the outside, somehow we will escape the tragedies of the soul. But each princess was tormented—persecuted, rejected, and abandoned by those who should have loved her the most. Little did I know that daring to live the fruit of the spirit—the true heart of a princess—would weave a life cluttered by betrayal, rejection, jealousy, and pain in female relationships.

But He knew.

If the world hates you, keep in mind that it hated me first. If you belonged to the world, it would love you as its own. As it is, you do not belong to the world, but I have chosen you out of the world. That is why the world hates you. Remember the words I spoke to you: No servant is greater than his master. If they persecuted me, they will persecute you also. If they obeyed my teaching, the will obey yours also. They will treat you this way because of my name, for they do not know the One who sent me. — John 15:18-21

So many of us women, desperate to live out the character planted in us by our Creator, have suffered tremendous wounds to our hearts. Journeying through the game of life we've often lost touch with which side we're on. Confused and conflicted by the demands for our time, attention, and passions, we've failed in relationships not only with the women around us, but in sacred friendships and primary bonds. We've allowed rejections and jealousies to form wounds in our hearts resulting in idols of identity—the ways in which we perceive or define our value. We've rejected traditional roles of femininity because we're afraid of being hurt and we believe walls and aggression are the ways we become strong.

As people, and as women specifically, we were made for community. Hardwired somewhere in the strands of our DNA is the desire for intimacy and closeness with other women. Without such relationships we are incomplete, and with them, there is hardship and heartache.

When the battle comes to our front door, we fear that the hatred is of us. We believe that we've done something wrong. We forget the battle wages all around us and is desperate for our soul. We forget that what is rejected is the One in us who was first left to die.

Searching for our wholeness every which way but Him, we're left feeling lost, insecure, afraid and alone. But it doesn't have to be this way any longer. We're looking back, but soon we're going to look in. And together we will journey into the hidden stories in our heart and find that what we've been looking for has been there all the while.

REFLECTION

- Has there been a time in your life, past or present, when you have rejected or renounced the notion or idea of being a princess? Why?

- If not, think back to some of your favorite childhood princesses or imagine a person or character that you did look up to as a young girl. What was it about her that captured you? As you look back with adult eyes, what do you see about her now that you didn't see then?

- What are some of the characteristics of a princess heart—the Fruit of the Spirit—that have been the hardest for you or have caused the most pain in your life?

- Looking back, was it worth it? How or why? What do you see now in your story that you didn't see or feel then?

2: PRETTY CONFUSING
Dante's Inferno, AKA Middle School

The greatest prison that people live in
is the fear of what other people think.
~David Icke

No sooner do we shove our confused notion of being a princess aside than we walk into the middle school hallways of a young woman's life. I affectionately refer to these years as my version of hell. At this point we're not at all sure who we are; but, we're pretty sure everyone else knows, and they don't like us one bit.

I remember my first days in the sixth grade knowing, with very little room for doubt, that I was not welcome. I got the feeling that just by walking through the front doors of the building I had somehow stepped onto some other girls' territory. And boy, were they going to let me know it.

As we enter the halls of our middle school years, a great war is raging for our young souls. Lost in a culture that lures us to pretty and then punishes us for falling in line, we are desperate to fit in but afraid of what that means.

Juggling the desires for a boyfriend with the demands for friendship, the rules of our parents against the war of our culture, and the internal fight for awareness and sense of self amidst the clamoring noise of our critics, we are propelled into one of the most difficult times of a young girl's life. Soon we begin to see the unraveling.

Friendships previously untouched by competition begin to wear thin. Gossip and meanness develops in young peer groups. Girls are excluded, whispered of in the hallways, and become the topic of secretly passed notes. Today it's even harder because we live in a world where a mean girl doesn't even have to have guts. When I grew up, a girl had to be seriously brave, or incredibly mean, to come square toe with you and tell you your place and what she planned to do to you if you stepped out of line. Either I lived in a small Midwest town where girls were brazen or I just had utterly bad luck, but I experienced this a few times with some strong and intimidating older girls. I learned pretty quickly to know my place, to not draw attention to myself, and to keep my head down when it came to the warnings they had given me.

In today's culture, a mean girl can blast her message to anyone bored enough to listen. Requiring no courage and incurring no consequences, she can post anonymously, bullying behind a computer and the safety of her own four walls. Her anger or malice doesn't know the boundaries of earshot and can grow and spread as far as a newsfeed status will take it.

People love a good fight. It's innate in our humanness, this competitive critical spirit. An angry outburst or mean-spirited attack seems to find much more momentum in this social-media driven world we live in—far more play than your average kind word of encouragement.

This is not a time for the faint of heart. It is not a time for the brave to grow weary. There is an enemy at work who knows our weaknesses, and for women, they are so often tied to acceptance—the invitation to a pretty girls' club, which we hate to remember, and yet know by heart.

Fearing we'll be rejected and hurt we begin warring against all that is pretty within us and begin clothing ourselves in the armor of independence, self-reliance, and protection.

Who are we? For most of us, we really don't know.

MADE FOR COMMUNITY

Take a moment and reflect on the landscape of women in your life. Consider your family, friends—near and dear or casual acquaintances. What is the community of women that surrounds you? What does it look like? How does it feel?

If you're anything like me it's been mixed company. As we journey together I will share personal stories and experiences as well as examples I've observed around me or have been blessed to have someone share with me. These stories are not to limit the scope of discussion to specific circumstances, but to illustrate the fiercely powerful relationships of women—how they can build and how they can destroy a spirit.

Much of my personal experience and observations of women in relationship reveal a competitiveness and superficiality that hides a hurt, broken, scarred, and bitter heart: daggers of jealousy thrown in misguided attempts at self-protection and self-preservation, never hitting the mark. Consider for a moment the woman at the school board meeting. I don't know who she is nor do I care to know her name, but I can almost guarantee she has known suffering and hardened her heart instead of choosing to remain soft. Her insult toward me only highlighted the fact that something in me ignited something in her that made her feel insecure or afraid. And she reacted.

We were made for community. We were made to live our lives better because of one another and because of our brokenness. But we've wandered from our greatest commandment to love because we're afraid we won't be loved in return, because we haven't been loved in return.

We're a broken people, each of us. Standing and falling with scraped up knees, not one of us makes it through this life unscathed. A world of broken, hurting people hurting other people, we must plan our course. But if the answer is always love, why do we endlessly search for another way?

IDENTITY

The road we are on is paved by identity. Searching for and uncovering the deepest and most beautiful question of your life: Who Am I?

The threads of identity will run throughout this journey because they are the strands that weave the tapestry of our lives. No matter what stage or season we're in, we continue to search for who we are—our best self. And life is a process of changing, evolving, searching for truth, forgetting, and remembering who we really are. We are not made to stay stagnant, but to grow as we discover what and who is inside of us. So, if we are made for community, in unity and diversity, how does that impact our identity?

At this stage of a young girl's life, it's a whole body experience. I look back on my middle school (and even some of high school) days as excruciating. I knew I was loved and cared for, and had some wonderful childhood friends, but I also knew I was rejected, ridiculed, and disliked by others. I was left out and whispered about in hallways.

When the kids would laugh and tell stories about events I wasn't invited to, I would pretend that I didn't care. But, really, it hurt. It felt like my whole identity was wrapped up in two small words: never enough.

I had some good friends growing up. But because there were popular girls who didn't want me to be included, many of my dearest friendships were outside of school, in secret. In school I mostly was treated well to my face (we'll talk more about that in Chapter 9), but I knew there was a boundary. Everyone walked a line. We all walk a line, don't we?

We know certain women who just don't get along. We know particular friends who have issues with other friends, and we figure out how to walk the line playing it safe with both sides. We think it's brave and wise to stay out of the middle of the bickering, but we show our true character by inaction. The noblest of friends stand up when someone is being treated poorly. The kindest gift you can give either friend is the truth.

At a young age, I figured out how to compartmentalize my sense of unworthiness around female friends. I learned to truly love my individual friendships and then wall up my heart so it didn't hurt when I wasn't invited to the parties. It worked in many ways for a long time, but it ultimately altered how I saw myself. I became hyper-critical of my actions, my words, my thoughts. I was extremely self-aware, and that made me hyper-aware of others too.

I learned very early on to watch body language and facial expressions, to read people and be discerning. So often, my young friends' actions didn't line up with their words. I learned to be intuitive and trust my heart because I saw through the illusion of pretty, and knew that what was happening under the surface was sometimes just plain dirty.

It began a journey of being very cautious in friendships with women. I can count on less than one hand the number of true friends I had growing up. To this day, I look back and there are only three I can say truly ever cared about me over the course of eighteen years. Three. In the end it teaches a girl a lot about discernment, but it took a long time to get there.

CODEPENDENCY AND RELATIONAL IDOLOTRY

During this time in our lives, our identities are completely rooted in our relationships. The conditions are perfect and we are prone to develop unhealthy patterns of codependency and relational idolatry. Believe me, I am the last person who wants to admit that I struggled with these issues but the truth is I probably always will. I bet you will too. It's the reality in which we live.

I remember the first time my mom told me I should read a book about codependency. I thought she was crazy. Codependency is commonly associated with addiction and enabling relationships. I was divorced. Single. Not even in a relationship! Surely this was not my problem. Unfortunately codependency's association with abusive or addictive relationships is so great that people tend to dismiss the control it has on each of our lives, whether in abusive or addictive relationships or not. What I've learned is being aware of it and accepting it is the first and most important hurdle to dealing with it.

In the context of this book, I am talking about codependency as a general pattern of behavior. In this regard, codependency is defined as dependence on the needs of another, or control by another.[1] We can be codependent to our husband or wife, of course, but we can also be codependent to a friend, child, colleague, boss or family member.

At first blush, codependency can seem to come from very well-meaning intentions. I remember being defensive of my behavior at first, trying to rationalize or explain it away as my overactive care or thoughtfulness of others. In actuality I was obsessed with their opinions of me. My mood and my day hinged on what others thought of me.

In most cases, a person struggling with codependency has a low or underdeveloped self-esteem, but that is not necessarily true. However, when you combine lack of self-esteem with an excessive sensitivity to others and an inappropriate reliance on another's response, you've got a perfect set up for codependent behavior.

In *Codependency for Dummies* Darlene Lancer, MFT, defines a codependent as someone "who can't function from his or her innate self, and instead, organizes thinking and behavior around a substance, process, or other person(s)."[2] If you're like me this feels a bit insulting at first blush. *Of course I can function from my innate self.* However, upon much longer reflection, I realized I actually couldn't.

Initially I was very averse to thinking I had any codependent tendencies. I thought it was only for people in abusive or addictive relationships, people with poor self-esteem or low self-worth. I was confident. Strong. Assertive. Happy. Yes, I was absolutely every one of those things. But I was also extremely codependent.

Have you ever found yourself obsessing about a particular person's opinion or thoughts of you? Has that obsession led you to change your behavior or act in a way other than you would normally? Or has there been something another person needed from you, but you weren't sure if you could or even wanted to help, yet you did anyway because you didn't want to let *them* down? There are a million little ways we can be, and are, codependent to someone else. Often we will find ourselves being codependent to our husbands, boyfriends, parents, siblings, and friends—especially those relationships where the person threatens to withhold something from us, or punish us if we don't perform. Those are especially rife with codependency. I believe our early experiences with codependency begin to create patterns of relational idolatry.

Relational idolatry happens when we get our identity tied up in someone else. When the relationship is going well, we feel good about ourselves. When it's not, we don't. I've seen this happen in both marriages and friendships and the result is the same. We serve a jealous God. Any time we are dealing with idolatry of any kind, it will be destroyed—not just challenged, but destroyed.

No single person can ever carry the entire weight of another. Though we may desire our husbands, family, or friends to meet our every need, the truth is it is just not possible. We are made to be in community. As individual parts of one body, with unique and diverse roles, we serve one another differently and together make up the whole. No one person can fulfill all roles. Trying would overwhelm and ultimately destroy the relationship. I can think of numerous people over the course of my life whom I made into idols. Their opinion, acceptance, and approval of me meant *everything*. Placing a person in a role that only God can fill will be destroyed every time. By necessity and by grace it cannot remain. Our identity can only be found in one place. Each of us, created in the image of a perfect God bears a gift, purpose, and light for such a time as this. Our identity rests not only in the knowledge, but in the firmly held belief that we were made by a Creator with every intention and purpose and plan to live this life well. To walk through, stumble over, and stand up stronger than we were before we started.

This life will try to break you. The people around you will fail you. But God is for you. And when you take your identity out of the hands of man and place it in the heart of God, you will find what you've been looking for.

REFLECTION

- What is your most difficult or painful middle school or teenage memory?

- How has it paved a road of identity, codependency, or relational idolatry in your life?

- What does the community of women around you look like right now? Is it safe?

- Does this community encourage and inspire you to become better? More truthful with yourself? More deeply connected to God?

- Being completely honest, how do you define yourself or where (or in whom) do you place your identity?

- Answer the question right now: Who Am I?

PART TWO
LOOKING IN

3: PRETTY BROKEN
Fear and Brokenness

This is the beginning of anything you want.
~Author Unknown

The older I get the more clearly I see we're dying. We hear news that someone we know has a terminal disease or was in a fatal accident, and we're heartbroken. We think, *Oh my God, why? How can this be?* In an instant we're taken on a fast-forward slideshow of our lives and wonder how it can be cut short in a moment? How can the panorama of a life change so dramatically in the breath of a few mere words?

In some ways it's a gift to know. It allows us the perspective we should have lived with from the start. My husband is a doctor who works with people in the very last days of life. He keeps patients alive and helps families make decisions about end stages and withdrawing care, giving dignity to death. He walks the hallways of the dying. He listens to the cries of the grieving and hears the moments of their deepest longing—the dying requests of a life unlived. But the truth is we're all terminal. We just don't know how long we have.

FEAR OF ABANDONMENT

Much of my life has been about fear. For me, it's always stemmed from a fear of abandonment and a deeply rooted fear that I was never enough—never smart enough, cool enough, funny enough to make the cut. I've always wanted to be included, to be *in* in a way that meant *all in*. I've always wanted to be all in.

Maybe you're like me and there's a deep place in your soul that wants to be known. You want to feel that despite all your flaws and the disgusting ugly parts that make you you, you're loved through all of it. You want to know that someone can look into you and see "the you" in you, and love you in spite of all the rest, because of all the rest. That, to me, is a true friend.

It's been a life mission and I'm pleased to say God has come through for me. He always comes through. But it wasn't without a lot of false starts, miles and miles of turbulence, and years of hard landings. Honestly, in so many ways, I'm still figuring out my landing gear.

Although I was probably considered a popular girl, I've always been on the fringe. My friends were the popular girls, and technically I had all the right things to make me fit in with the popular crowd, but I was a complete outsider too. A part of me always felt like I was looking in; I just had a front row seat.

My heart didn't always line up with what was popular. My mind was always playing catch up to what was considered cool. I look back on much of my life and it feels as though I was missing the punch line. For some reason, what seemed so funny to everyone around me just didn't seem very funny to me. At all.

A man I admire once told me that the lowest form of humor is that which comes at the expense of someone else. It was like hearing words put to the dead silences of the punch lines of my life. We live in a world where sarcasm is king. We laugh at nothing more than a cheap shot at someone else's expense. It comes from a place of hostility rather than authenticity or creativity.

The word sarcasm comes from the ancient Greek "to tear flesh, gnash the teeth, speak bitterly." Its first definition is "a sharp, bitter, or cutting expression or remark, a bitter gibe or taunt."[3]

DEATH TO SARCASM

Unfortunately, more often than not, it seems we live in a world and a time where it is cooler to be mean, nasty, and cynical than it is to hope. The reckless few who dare to dream, to be hope-spreaders and grace-givers are ridiculed as do-gooders with the full eye-roll. The ones brave enough to stand apart from the crowd and sing a different tune? We laugh at them. We crack jokes and post seemingly innocuous updates on our Facebook status when we're really just being mean.

Why is it that we give some people the power to control the dialogue? Perhaps it's because they're bolder than most, and louder than the rest. They say things that are hurtful and snide and belittling and rude and we're afraid to disagree. We don't want them to think we're rude; we don't want to offend *them*. So we join in the banter or silently stand alongside, condoning the behavior. Like the girls who quietly stand on the sidelines while another one gets broken, we don't actively participate in the assault, but we certainly don't intervene.

We do it on purpose, and we do it without even knowing it, and the result is the same. We cannot feign ignorance anymore. Sometimes the same women who cry out anti-bullying rhetoric for daughters in our schools are guilty of swinging the same sword in their own lives. People like me. People like you.

We hurt one another because of our own embroiled bitterness, fear, insecurity, and pain. Many of us pretend we're okay when we're really just experts at holding grudges, and we secretly harbor ill will.

For every snide comment on Facebook making a sarcastic joke of a generic group of people, there is a woman who just found out her husband has been having an affair or a woman who just lost her mother to cancer or a woman who lost her child in a horrible tragedy who may see that comment and take it personally. Perhaps she shut down her computer, shuffled back to her bed, threw the covers over her head, feeling even worse about her sorry, sad life than she did before. For a joke? It's not funny.

And that woman, the one lost in a sea of despair who heard our joke making fun of her life? She'll look at each of us differently. And she'll have a right to because it hurts. Life hurts and then we hurt each other more in the middle of our suffering.

We kid ourselves when we think this world is about us and that we can post what we want, say what we want, do what we want, and not think it will affect someone else's life. We cannot keep talking out both sides of our mouths—demanding protection for our daughters and then carelessly slamming our friends—and say that it's all in fun. *It's just a joke.* Well it's not funny.

We don't live in the same world we grew up in where a joke went only as far as the handful of friends who heard it. Today we publish. Every one of us a writer. We publish on Facebook; we publish on blogs; we have the power to mass disseminate any information we want because we just happen to be in a bad mood. It's a dangerous time to be misunderstood. It is a dangerous time to stand apart. And yet, it is why we must do just that.

We live in a time where we are being bombarded with messages about identity, expectations, and the competitive dance for worthiness every minute of every day. We navigate a web of mixed messages telling us to be ourselves, be true to who we are, be who God made us to be. Then our own family, friends, or people we respect and trust take us out at the knees.

People will shock us with their unexpected participation in an age-old game that mean girls play—a game, like the one I was invited to by the woman at the school board meeting. It's the same game that's been played for a long time by those too afraid to stand apart from the status quo and rise up for the dignity of the hurting; those reluctant to make room for the quiet voice of the real. To fight for those who silently walk alongside us, many of whom we selfishly refuse to see, that are slowly dying inside.

Blessed are the poor in spirit, for theirs is the kingdom of heaven. Blessed are those who mourn, for they will be comforted. Blessed are the meek, for they will inherit the earth. Blessed are those who hunger and thirst for righteousness, for they will be filled. Blessed are the merciful, for they will be shown mercy. Blessed are the pure in heart, for they will see God. Blessed are the peacemakers, for they will be called children of God. Blessed are those who are persecuted because of righteousness, for theirs is the kingdom of heaven. Blessed are you when people insult you, persecute you and falsely say all kinds of evil against you because of me. Rejoice and be glad, because great is your reward in heaven.   —Matthew 5:1-12

The way I see it, we live in a time when not only should we intervene, we have a responsibility and a call to do so, not in anger or harshness, not repaying in kind, but in truth and in love.

> You are the light of the world. A town built on a hill cannot be hidden. Neither do people light a lamp and put it under a bowl. Instead they put it on its stand, and it gives light to everyone in the house. In the same way, let your light shine before others, that they may see your good deeds and glorify your Father in heaven.
> —Matthew 5:14-16

I think one of the biggest fears women face is the fear of standing apart. Whether we go along with the person or group even when we disagree or hide in the cover of a crowd because we don't want the attention, we're afraid. That fear can make us feel small, manifesting as insecurity, distrust, compliance, and indecisiveness. It can also make us feel deceptively big, revealing itself as pride, arrogance, control, and false modesty. What or who are you afraid of?

SHARED BROKENNESS

As women we are made to go deep and yet we live on the surface of life. Years of pain and brokenness have taught us to put up walls to protect our hearts. On the surface, the average eye can look at our life and see beauty—a successful husband, well-mannered children, a tidy home, and a big fake smile on our pretty-made faces. How could they know we're dying inside?

How could they know that our marriage is broken or we're secretly afraid of our husband? How could they imagine we go home to drink just to deal with our day? How could they see that inside we wish we had married someone else, that our husband has been cheating on us for years, or that he's hitting the kids and we don't know what to do. How could they tell that we're angry and bitter and taking it out on our children? In secret, we lie, steal, cheat to get ahead. We're terrible gossips and secretly love nothing more than seeing someone else fail or fall. Beneath all the pretty veneers, how could they ever know how broken we really are?

The most dangerous lie we can ever tell ourselves is that it doesn't matter and we don't care that we're broken. We convince ourselves that what's broken can never be healed because we just don't care anymore. But the truth is we were made to care. Made in the image and likeness of a God who came to love, we care deeply. Saying we don't care never settles in our spirit because it can't. It keeps erupting, forcing us to deal with its tension because it is antithetical to our being. We are compelled to bare our brokenness and find healing in the very act of dying to this fallen world.

The truth of our healing lies in the courage to reach out, the strength to stand in the middle of our mess and say, "Here I am, choose me." We may not get picked. But what if we don't? I mean seriously. So what if we don't? Isn't it better not to be accepted *by this world?* Maybe what we really want to say is, here I am, *see* me. Don't pick me. Don't judge me, don't choose me. Just *see* me. See my beauty and see my brokenness, and see me, all of me, beautiful me. Please, just see.

It reminds me of a scene with Jack Frost in the children's movie *The Rise of the Guardians*. No one has ever believed in him and so he has walked his life unseen. Toward the end of the film a little boy stands in his room, the last holdout to believe in the guardians; but, after a disastrous Easter, his faith is waning. In the scene, Jack is trying to make him believe in the Easter Bunny. He makes a bunny from frost on the window and brings it to life, jumping and dancing around the little boy, and fills his room with delicate falling snow.

The little boy's eyes are filled with wonder as he turns in a circle in the room, taking it all in. He whispers "Jack Frost," and for the first time Jack hears his name spoken aloud. His whole body fills with the thrill of recognition and he responds to the boy, "Yes, yes, it's me! Jack Frost!" The little boy's eyes widen as he stares silently at Jack Frost, who responds, "Wait, can you see me?" The little boy nods, eyes full of wonder, as Jack laughs and smiles and jumps as his spirit soars, filled with the overwhelming sense of being known, *seen* for who he is. Finally real.

We all just want to be seen—known for who we really are—no expectations, no grand delusions, just seen. Have the eyes to see those around you who are dying inside. Give honor by saying, "I see you. I know. I'm hurting too." Together we can walk this life well; we aren't made to go alone.

But we've been hurt. We've been rejected and abandoned and had cruel things done to us and had people make jokes out of us. So we're scared. And because of our hurt, we close ourselves off from the world, pretending we're okay. Living on the surface of a superficial life we try to persuade ourselves that we're okay, that life is okay, and sometimes it's just not. We see our friends and acquaintances in the course of our day and we say, "We're good, life's good, we're fine. Kids are great, life is great." And the truth is we're broken—broken people living broken lives, pretending it's good. Fine. But the house falls in.

Wrecked from within, the tired roof caves down and the walls fall in. Windows shatter and knife sharp shards of glass pierce the lives of all who live inside. What took so long to build, is destroyed in a moment by our very own hands.

What if we lived in the open? What if we shared our brokenness as if it were the very thing that could give us life? What if we cared enough to splay ourselves open for the sake of our healing? What if we risked everything we thought the world held as right—the image of a perfect life—and were honest that it's not good. *No, we're not fine.* We're terminal.

Only through the lens of our shared brokenness do we see that we are better together—the tapestry woven of the finest fabric of the human experience: unconditional love, pain, joy, tragedy, and the enduring faithfulness of a Heavenly Father who offers us wholeness.

If you feel broken, take heart; you're in good company. Remind yourself God is for you, with great plans to prosper you. Do not break in your brokenness. Do not harden your heart or erect walls of shame, insecurity, hatred, and revenge.

I truly believe that every trial we face is meant for our refinement, and though I don't welcome them at the time, I'm thankful for each and every one. We are only as strong as our greatest weakness, and we've all got them. The question is whether we admit them, talk about them, grow through them, and let them change us . . . or allow them to limit our strength. I'm not willing to let my fear keep me small. This journey is about being bold.

Boldness demands that we live our lives with intention or we risk missing the point. The inevitability of this life is that we will have trial, we will face pain, and we will be tempted to lose heart. But we have a choice. We can be bold and brave, and we can face our adversaries and speak truth and love. We can allow the hurt to make us stronger and the lies weaker. We can unshackle ourselves from those things that try to hold us back. We can design our lives free from bondage and boldly live unhindered lives. But first we've got to be real. It's the birthplace of freedom.

Unclench your fist, open your hands, and let Him work. He is building you strong. He is making you whole. And somewhere down the road of grace you will look back and see redemption's clear story; and you'll be grateful that it happened just the way that it did. You are beautiful.

REFLECTION

- What or who are you afraid of?

- What is your biggest fear?

- Have you been involved in a situation where you were abandoned or ridiculed by a person or group? Or were you a perpetrator? How did it make you feel? How did you move forward?

- What are you hiding under the surface of your pretty life? Do you have someone safe with whom you can share your brokenness?

- What does living in the open mean to you?

- How can you better begin to "see" others around you?

4: PRETTY SHALLOW
Made to Go Deep

What lies behind us and what lies before us
are tiny matters compared to what lies within us.
~Ralph Waldo Emerson

In 2012 I completed the Coeur d'Alene Ironman. For those unfamiliar with the sport of triathlon, an Ironman is a 140.6-mile race. It begins with a 2.4-mile swim, followed by a 112-mile bike ride, concluding with a 26.2-mile run. It was, and is, the greatest achievement of my athletic career so far. You have seventeen hours to complete the race, and incremental times are required for completing the swim and bike portions. I finished after 13.5 hours of consecutive endurance, pushing my body to extremes that seem impossible. And yet is . . . possible.

IRONMAN SWIM

Toes barely touching the water, I look out at the horizon. The mountains cast their shadows deep into the lake; a cloudy grey sky threatens rain. We link arms, my brother and I. Barefoot, we stand on the beach—a bond about to be forged in the deep, cold water and the miles we are about to travel this Ironman day. We gaze in silent surrender to that distant place. Knowing, and yet not knowing, what lies before us.

Adrift in the moment, we lose track of time. A cannon fires and we dive. A mass of bodies pierces the stillness of the once calm lake. A thundering storm erupts beneath the water and my brother and I are separated. Calm, silent surrender is immediately overtaken by panic and fear. Alone. Kicking, thrashing, drowning, it's happening. I'm going to die.

I roll onto my back coughing water out of my lungs and stare fixedly at the clouded sky. As if looking directly into the Father's eyes, I cry out: *Lord, where are you? Please. Help.*

An army of arms closing behind me, I turn quickly and begin my stroke. Stay calm. One, two, three, breathe. One, two, breathe. Rhythm, timing, uninterrupted in prayer: *Lord, go before me. Make a way.*

Much of life can feel like drowning. Arms flailing, legs kicking, we struggle to get our heads above water. Pushed and pulled down by others trying to get by, to get ahead. We coach ourselves one, two, three, breathe. One, two, breathe.

So many times we're scared to leave the safety of the shore or we stay in the comfort of the shallows. But we're called to go deep.

We believe if we train hard enough or practice long enough, we will succeed on our own. That hours spent in the pool will help us when we face open water. But when the water gets deep and our feet no longer touch, we realize that our strength is not enough. Our weakness becomes frighteningly real as we face the unforgiving depths of the darkness.

For me, nothing captures the faithfulness of God like my swim on Ironman morning. People ask, "What was it like?" I pause because there's no way to describe it without sharing the intimate presence of a faithful Father. Among thousands of bodies equally frightened and terrified of drowning; He went before me. Opening a narrow channel in a sea of thrashing bodies, He made a way.

In that moment I realized we are companions of fear, each of us afraid to unclench our fists and surrender to the One who knows the depths of our souls, who hears the desperate cries of our hearts. We know this, and yet we struggle to believe it is true. We resist believing it for *us*. And we're faced with the paradox that we cannot fully rest in Him if we don't follow Him into deep water.

In life and in love, how deep do you go? For most of us, we're just skimming the surface of a superficial life—desperate to be known but afraid to go deep. We long for it, and yet it is our biggest fear.

SHALLOW WATERS

What are you afraid of? It's just you here, I promise. Even I can't hear, so just lay it all out there. (We'll talk more about being truthful with ourselves in Chapter 7.) So often, when I think the whole world is watching or listening, I remember that I'm just sitting alone in my bed reading my book and it's just me. *It's just you.*

We live in a time when everyone is so connected and interwoven, and everything is so very public that the world seems small. We start to believe everyone's looking at us, and they can see that we're running ragged trying to keep up with all the demands and expectations on us, trying to keep everything from falling apart. We're afraid they can see all that we try so hard to hide.

And we're tired. We're not who we pretend to be. When we're alone in our house in the still of the night we feel like a fraud, an imposter parading around in a pretty, put-together life. But it's only skin-deep.

The reality is we're all just one moment from falling apart. We're just one new diet away from feeling fit and thin, just an outfit away from feeling stylish and up to date, a Botox shot away from feeling youthful and smart, and just one more cosmetic surgery away from feeling truly beautiful. So we put it on the credit card, hide it in the closet, and hope that this is our thing. Our last attempt to make us whole. Pretty.

We pray for it to deliver the fullness of beauty and grace and timelessness that we've been promised and that our culture has led us to believe is wholeness. But the fix won't take. The fix can't take, because we were made for more than pretty.

And in our paranoia we think that everyone can see our struggle because we forget that the world is big. We forget that everyone is immersed in the same battle—living on the surface of a superficial life—pretending it's okay, pretending we're okay. And we're not. So just sit for a minute in a room without sound and ask yourself: *How are you? How is your heart? Are you where you want to be? Are you who you want to be?*

There's a superficial peace that lies on the surface of our daily lives, but it haunts our spirits at night. I'm not a gambler, but I'd put down money that you're tired—tired of acting, tired of playing a part that you were never meant to play in a life you were never made to live.

SUPER(FICIAL) HEROES

In 2012 the annual revenue of the United States weight-loss industry was over $20 billion. Over 108 million people were on diets, and about 85% of them were women.[4] Upwards of 6% of the U.S. adult population shops compulsively, and most are women.[5] In 2012 the American Society for Aesthetic Plastic Surgery (ASAPS) reported over 10 million cosmetic procedures by certified doctors in the United States. Of the 10 million cosmetic procedures, 9.1 million were female patients.[6] Americans spent almost $11 billion on cosmetic procedures in 2012. That's $11,000,000,000.00. Of that total, $6.7 billion was spent on surgical procedures; $2 billion was spent on injectable enhancements; $1.8 billion was spent on skin rejuvenation; and over $483 million was spent on other nonsurgical procedures, including laser hair removal and treatment of leg veins.[7]

Probably the most stunning statistic comes from the American Academy of Facial and Reconstructive Surgery (AAFPRS) that reports social media may be driving an increase in plastic surgery requests. In an annual poll, they surveyed 752 of the AAFPRS's board-certified facial plastic surgeons on the trends in reconstructive surgery. In 2012, one finding stands out: surgeons are seeing a 31% increase in cosmetic procedures specifically as a result of patients wanting to look more attractive *on social media*.[8]

MEASURELESS LOVE

Who or what holds the measuring tape in your life? What person or industry sets the standard you strive to attain? Who defines what beauty, style, and image means in your life?

We serve a God who tells us we cannot measure His love—a God meticulous with measurement. This is the same God who set the earth just the right distance from the sun, the same God who placed the stars and galaxies in their exact locations. Planned. Placed. Measured. Exact. All so we would not burn up and die in a raging inferno. That God—THE God—tells us we cannot measure His radical, unfailing love.

> I pray that out of his glorious riches he may strengthen you with power through his Spirit in your inner being, so that Christ may dwell in your hearts through faith. And I pray that you, being rooted and established in love, may have power, together with all the saints, to grasp how wide and long and high and deep is the love of Christ, and to know this love that surpasses knowledge – that you may be filled to the measure of all the fullness of God.   — Ephesians 3:16-19

Not only is His love measureless, we cannot grasp it—cannot understand its breadth—without power from the saints. That only by being rooted and established in love can we grasp how *wide*, how *long*, how *high*, and how *deep* is the love of Christ.

We are rooted and established in the measureless love of God! Which begs the question: Who or what are you trying to measure up to? Who or what are you trying to measure up for? Are we trying to fulfill man's perception of beauty or grace, *pretty* or popular, or are we trying to please God? We will become an all-out servant to whatever we are trying to please. God has come to tend to our inner being, to strengthen us with power through His Spirit in our *inner being* so we may be filled to the measure of all the fullness of God—all the fullness of God, which is immeasurable! No earthly measure can capture what He fills in us, what He does through us, what He has already done for us.

PERCEPTION IS REALITY

In 1985 an advertising agency launched one of the most successful campaigns of the '80s for *Rolling Stone* magazine. The ad concept: perception vs. reality.

Here, they challenged the perception of the magazine's poor, aging, hippie audience, juxtaposing it against the reality of their spending habits, tastes, and influence. Here, perception fell far from reality.

I would argue today's ad campaigns continue to draw from the genius of the campaign addressing the relationship between perception and reality, but it has been perverted from its original form. Used in a culture so wholly warped by media, the creative originality has since been used to cause harm. Every ad campaign rests on the underlying foundation of perception versus reality, but no longer is the goal to delineate the disparity between perception and reality and to prove the point that the reality is so much better. The truth we have come to accept in this modern world is that perception *is* reality.

If we look pretty, act pretty, talk pretty, and dress pretty then we are, by this culture's definition, pretty. We've come to value an illusion of pretty that doesn't even exist. We've wrapped ourselves in a pretty package while being broken inside, wondering what we did wrong. We followed the rules and we still don't *feel* pretty. We still don't believe we're beautiful.

ABC reports the average salaries paid to celebrity endorsers of major weight-loss programs is $500,000 to $3 million. On average, a celebrity endorser earns $33,000 per pound lost.[9] It's a business—a business geared to making women believe they are less than what they should be. They come to believe they will never be enough and that their external beauty defines their internal worth. It's a lie.

They take your money and pay celebrities billions of dollars to make you feel bad about yourself. And those women are just as broken as you are. They struggle with the same failures, insecurities, jealousies, and pain as you. We cannot change from the outside in. The change we most desire—to find love and value in ourselves, as ourselves—has to come from the inside out.

My point really isn't so much about shopping, dieting, or plastic surgery; it's just an easy target. My desire is not to provoke you, but to awaken you. Most of us have tried some kind of crazy diet. Many of us have had plastic surgery or skin procedures, and many more of us wish we could. It's really a personal decision. I'm not saying that the choice to pursue a diet or procedure is wrong or highlights an emotional, psychological, or spiritual weakness. Not at all.

The concern is the underlying reason for the diet, procedure, or shopping spree. A problem begins when we don't believe we are good enough the way we are and when we believe our happiness, our worth, or our value will come as a result of changing our external appearance. We have been lured into the trap of excess and more, believing that *if* we were twenty pounds lighter *then* we could be happy. *If* we had a better wardrobe, *then* we would be included with that group of popular women. *If* we had a more perfect shape, or the right nose, or a flatter stomach, *then* we would be beautiful.

It stems from a belief system that says if we look pretty then somehow we can avoid pain. The problem occurs when we place the surgery, weight loss, or fashionable wardrobe above ourselves, above the beauty that is intrinsic to our being—when we place the external above the internal. First, we must know we are enough and we will not be magically *more enough* as a result of a cosmetic change. You are enough. Just as you are, you are enough. His love for you, His care for you, His adoration over you is measureless. He delights in you. You are beautiful.

IMPERATIVE INVESTMENT

There is a war over our souls. I believe with every fiber of my being that as we walk this earth, we are crossing a battlefield with an enemy who will stop at nothing to exploit our weaknesses.

Imagine your home for a moment. Perhaps you close your eyes and see the house you thought you would live in, tucked in the simple memory of a child: lush green grass and a white clapboard house. A swing hangs on the front porch. A white picket fence gracefully lines the perimeter of the yard. It is peaceful. Serene. As you scan the horizon and look out to the fields in the neighboring parcel you notice a part of the fence has fallen down. It's not totally broken, but you can see a few of the boards have fallen loose or were damaged from some kind of impact or trauma.

You look to the other end of the property and another part is rotted through. The walls erected to keep bad things out—or keep good things in—are no longer sure. Through the trials of life, unresolved pain, and misplaced identity, we find that our walls or our fences are not entirely secure. We falsely believed we were safe.

The enemy watches our fences. He scans the horizon of our lives, looking for loose or damaged boards—a sliver of space where he can slip in and breed doubt. He seeks to stir dissention, whisper lies, and create chaos. This is the place where your greatest dream meets your darkest fear, where your joy meets your sorrow. These are the places only you know, the vulnerability tucked so deeply in the recesses of your heart, conceived out of the pages of the story of your life.

It is why there is an urgent call on our lives to tend to the deep internal places of our hearts and to make the imperative investment in our soul. No one can do it but us, and no promises of greatness are included in the package. The journey is not easy and requires perseverance, faith, and good old-fashioned work.

We live in a culture that has lost the ethic of work. Lost in the wave of reality television, many in the culture today believe they can be lazy and selfish and still entitled to everything. Their greatest ambition is to be rich and famous. But they don't know how to work, let alone work hard.

We're going to have to dig deep and work hard to fight for the health of our souls, especially in the world we live in today. It's getting darker and meaner every single day, but there is still light! I promise you, there is so much light.

Make the imperative investment. Seek out the dark places of your heart. Find where the boards have come loose or fallen down along your fence and work to rebuild them strong. Seek healing from your Maker. Invest in your heart, your mind, your body, and your soul. It's not easy work. There are no gimmicks or simple promises. If there are, you know it's a lie.

Real change comes from aligning ourselves on the inside and that takes walking the fence line—one by one, repairing the broken damaged pieces of a life. Piece by piece, you rebuild hope, truth, relationship, and faith. It's our life's work, because we were made to go deep.

Our greatest hurts lie in the deepest darkest places of our souls. Some of them we've denied for so long we've forgotten they're even there. But they haven't. They haven't lost or forgotten their power. Remember, we are only as strong as our greatest weakness. Don't let your fear keep you small!

Don't let it win the battle over your soul.

You were made to go to deep places and He will meet you there. As with my Ironman swim, I believe He will find us in the place where we can no longer rely on our own understanding or strength. He will meet us where we must believe in something bigger and greater than ourselves, when we realize He is all we need, that He is all we've ever needed.

REFLECTION

- How are you? Really, how *are* you? Are you who you want to be? Are you where you want to be?

- What is your super(ficial) hero?

- Who or what holds the measuring tape in your life?

- Where are the broken, vulnerable places in your life and heart? What are the cracks or broken boards in the fence where you are weak?

- Where do you find yourself stumbling time and time again?

- How can you begin repairing these vulnerable places? What is one step or one way you will commit to today?

5: PRETTY VICES
The Art of Distraction

Freedom is a possession of inestimable value.

~Cicero

The last few years have been a journey of identity. I've been convicted by my thoughts, values, and the ways I have lived, as well as the way I still find myself living so much of the time. I am realizing the power I have given so freely to others over my life: my actions, thoughts, and feelings. The idols we make of other people and their acceptance and inclusion, the idols we make of things and where we place our value all factor into the identity we form.

What gives us satisfaction and value? Where do we find ourselves complaining, hurting, and grieving time and again? In those places we find our hearts. For, where we dwell, our heart can be found. More often than not, I must admit my heart is found in selfishness and vain conceit. Striving for approval, affection, and significance. My heart is distracted by the world. It's so easy to be distracted by this world.

Pick your poison. There's a perfect temptation for each of us—one seemingly hand-crafted by the tormentor of our spirit. He studies our broken down fence so carefully for the places he can sneak in and destroy. He waits for the perfect timing—when we're lonely, afraid, or weak—and he whispers into the deep places of our longing.

So many of us don't know who we are. We see ourselves only through the reflection of other people's eyes, leaving us vulnerable to the lies of the world. What do they think of us? Who do they think we are? Are we significant to them? Distracted by others, we forget what *we* think. We forget who God says we are. We forget to keep searching for God in us—our truest self.

We're a nation so rich, and yet so very poor. We suffer from a poverty of spirit so deep, we're willing to search for anything in this world to fill the emptiness.

ADDICTION TO DISTRACTION

For many of us, the seemingly innocent distractions—things like the Internet, television, email, shopping, decorating, and food—fill the void. These are fundamentally helpful things that, when used to excess, become distractions from life and living. They keep us distant from God, our families, and truly knowing ourselves.

Why do we continue to shop when our husbands have told us we can't afford it? Why do we eat when we're not even hungry? Why do we spend hours on the Internet and social media sites while our kids keep asking us to play?

I'm guilty of these things too much of the time.

How often do we turn on the television or sit at our computers to escape the reality of our own lives? Reality TV seems to have become our preferred reality. It is an empty void of life, a complete waste of time, and yet it brings a mindless, effortless comfort. We are numbing ourselves from that which is real in our lives—the things we don't want to deal with, the complaints we don't want to be bothered with, the arguments we don't want to have, the noise we don't want to hear.

We use television, Internet, and our smart phones to escape the present moment. We're so tired of our lives and unwilling to do the work to make them better, so we numb out. We tune out; we check out; and we miss out.

Many are addicted to social media—Facebook, Pinterest, Instagram, and Twitter. We quiet the chaos of our lives by tuning into the newsfeed of our choice. For some, it's gossip or social climbing. We hide our true selves and put on a new costume. We distract our hearts from our own problems and get our nose into everyone else's business. We set up lunch dates, girls' weekends, and fill idle moments with gossip while we bond over critical spirits. For others, there are bigger distractions with much deeper wounds and secrets. We struggle with addiction to alcohol, drugs, or sex. We're lost in a world that is no longer our own and one we can no longer control by our own strength. And it's killing us— silently, but effectively, killing us and the ones we love the most.

It's happening all around us. It is hidden in the person you pass in the supermarket aisle, the woman you see at the coffee shop, the top executive at your company, the janitor at the school, the pastor at your local church, and the stay-at-home mom. None of us are immune to the lures of this dark world. None of us is equipped with the weapons to defend ourselves from the lies and temptation of an overly sexualized, self-absorbed, sinful culture.

So we shove our distractions and addictions down into the darkest places inside of us where no one can see. We fool ourselves into believing that as long as it all looks pretty on the outside no one will ever know. But we know. The enemy of our soul knows. And he exploits us. After all, he lied to us in the beginning, and now he's got us in shame. He plays a vicious, vicious game, hell-bent on destroying the fabric of our souls.

But if shame lives in the dark, then we know the solution is to bring it into the light. But we're so afraid, so terribly, unbearably afraid to be real. We are afraid to be vulnerable and expose our sin nature because deep down we believe we're not worthy of love. At some point in our pasts we were thrown away by someone who was supposed to love us, and we believed it was our fault. We believed we did something to deserve it, and we're afraid it will happen again. So we numb. And we seek comfort in escape, addiction, or the arms of another.

We distract ourselves from the pain that hides in the very core of our spirits because we believe if we just keep pushing it down we can run from it. If we can ignore it long enough, it will stop talking. We believe that eventually the quiet voice of the spirit will forget how to speak and we'll be free.

And so we live in a perpetual state of an unlived life. We live only to the boundary of our walls, addictions, and lies. We are caught up in the lie that perception equals reality and we're only fooling ourselves. And, no one else has the time to see that we're dying inside because they're busy being distracted by the very same game. So the only one we're hurting is ourselves.

And with every passing day, with every false crutch, we distance ourselves further from our true self. We slip further from the God that lives in us, further from the healing and wholeness that lies just on the other side of our fear.

CHOOSING HOPE

Eventually we discover we cannot fix what's broken in us. Discouraged by the solutions of this world we are left confused and lonely. We grow impatient. In a life so full of instant gratification we're unaccustomed to waiting for God to tend to our hearts while truth slowly filters in and for time to show us the lesson deeply imbedded in the trial. We struggle to find an answer—any answer—so we can understand.

But sometimes, there is no understanding what has happened to us. The life we've lived and the pain we've endured cannot, and will not, ever make sense. We want an answer. Truth or lie—it doesn't matter as long as we aren't left with questions. But sometimes all we have are the fragments of a life and no way to fit them together.

This is when we must choose hope, because hope is a "revolutionary patience."[10] It begins in the darkest places in the times we feel utterly lost and alone. It is where confusion reigns, and instead of shrinking down in the spiral of self-doubt and discouragement, we speak truth to the lies that come for our peace. We find the strength to stand, cradled in a stubborn hope that believes if we show up, if we do the right thing, the dawn will come and light will break onto the horizon. The warmth of its truth will penetrate our soul and fill us with peace. The light will teach us to be patient, will show us that we do not face this world alone, and that we are better for the heartache. We are comforted by the truth that this is not our home.

Praise be to our God and Father. In His great mercy has given us new birth into a living hope through the resurrection of Jesus Christ from the dead, and into an inheritance that can never perish, spoil or fade – kept in heaven for you, who through faith are shielded by God's power until the coming of the salvation that is ready to be revealed in the last time.

In this you greatly rejoice, though now for a little while you may have had to suffer grief in all kinds of trials. These have come so that your faith – of greater worth than gold, which perishes even though refined by fire – may be proved genuine and may result in praise, glory and honor when Jesus Christ is revealed.   —1 Peter 1:3-7

Our lives are a constant refining process where we are stripped of ourselves, stripped of the things we cling to in this life. Health, relationships, possessions, and security can be taken in a moment. We are caught unaware. Without faith we are left in confusion, disbelief, heartache, and despair. We fall prey to the lies and doubt competing to fill the void in our hearts. Addictions and distractions become our comfort, and so we must turn to hope.

We must turn to faith: the belief in something for which there is no proof. This life is hard. This life brings so much pain. We must believe we were made for more and that is why it hurts so badly. With souls made for eternity, sometimes it breaks our hearts to live in this world.

Let the trials of this life prove your faith genuine—real, true, authentic, sincere—so your life will match your heart, and your heart will match your faith.

MOVE

As a runner, I firmly believe that we must move physically in order for our lives to move emotionally or mentally. Physical fitness and pushing my body to its absolute limits has been my greatest catalyst for growth and healing and I cannot deny its power.

Pushing my body to run and train and extend beyond the confines of what I believed I could do—or what I even wanted to do—has crafted in me much more than endurance. Far more than a collection of shiny medals, it has rewarded me with the understanding that I have very little control over anyone else in this life. As an athlete, the only person I can improve is myself. I don't get to take out my competitor or push them down to make me better. I show up. I do the work, day in and day out, and focus on what I can change, how I can move, and where I need to grow. As an athlete I need to surround myself with people better and smarter and fitter and faster than I am because I need their strength to find my own. I need their best to push me to find my best.

> Therefore, since we are surrounded by such a great cloud of witnesses, let us throw off everything that hinders and the sin that so easily entangles. And let us run with perseverance the race marked out for us, fixing our eyes on Jesus, the author and perfecter of faith. [Who] for the joy set before him endured the cross, scorning its shame, and sat down at the right hand of the throne of God. Consider him who endured such opposition from sinful men, so that you will not grow weary and lose heart. —Hebrews 12:1-4

What does it mean to be hindered?

A hindrance is something that makes slow or difficult the progress of; or holds us back.[11] Have you ever had a moment when you were moving along totally unaware, and something from your past—a loss, hurt, fear, failure, regret—just literally came out of nowhere and sent you reeling before you knew what hit you? It's happened to me, and more often than I'd like I take a total face plant. If you look farther down the definition you can see that a hindrance can also be described as a fetter, handcuff, handicap, hog-tie, or shackle. It is stress that causes harmful or annoying delay or interference with progress. Put that way, it's amazing how many hindrances we live with every single day.

I think about the verse from Hebrews, and the imagery both challenges and inspires me. From the start, we are given hope to hold onto the promise that we are surrounded by a great cloud of witnesses. We are surrounded by all those who faithfully have gone before us in the Heavenly realms who stand with us and for us. We come to learn that nothing in this life is meant for our harm; and the trial and troubles that torment us are part of our refinement, part of proving us genuine.

Holding to that promise, we are to throw off everything that hinders and the sin that entangles. We are to run with perseverance the race set before us. Each one of us has been given a race to run in this life: a passion, mission, gift, calling, or purpose *for such a time as this.* This imagery illustrates both a throwing off and a running toward. We run *from* that which we have thrown off—our vices, distractions, addictions, unhealthy behaviors, relationships and attitudes—and run *to* the race God has called in our lives, all that is pure, good, healthy, life giving, and true.

This life is a marathon. And as with all marathons, there are times when the miles get tough. There are times we have to dig in and find the sum of all that of which we're made. We search for strength, rooted in a stubborn hope that believes that if we do the work and keep on fighting, we will find the strength of Him who lives in us.

Each of us knows the areas of our lives that have become unmanageable—the areas where, despite all our best efforts, we cannot refrain from sin. We cannot resist the distraction or temptation. We know, and yet we deceive ourselves. Now is the time to throw off what hinders—the things robbing us of healing and standing between us and God, the lies that haunt us and continue to numb our lives.

He promises to take these heavy burdens from us if we would lay them at the cross, if we would run with perseverance this great marathon race, alive and vulnerable, unhindered and free. He called us to live a life of purpose—a purpose no one else can fulfill. But we have to unhinder ourselves from the shackles of fear and the chains of addictions and lies. We have to unburden ourselves by stepping out of our *preferred* realities and into *our* realities. His grace is sufficient.

> My grace is sufficient for you, for my power is made perfect in weakness. Therefore I will boast all the more gladly about my weaknesses, so that Christ's power may rest on me. For when I am weak, then I am strong.
> —2 Cor. 12:7-10

He knows our trials, the thorns buried deep in our flesh. He allows us to carry them so we will seek Him, so His power might be manifested in our greatest weakness. Stop numbing. Stop distracting from what grows in the dark. Turn on the light and find the strength to stand. Throw off what hinders and find your race.

We don't all have to run, but we do need to move—not from our pasts, but to our futures. Find the strength that lies buried in the shadow of your greatest fear and move. In whatever way you know how, move.

REFLECTION

- What is your greatest hindrance or distraction?

- How has this distraction kept you from coming face to face with whatever it is in you that needs healing?

- How have you seen the process of refinement in your story? Even though it was painful, would you trade it for an easier path? Why or why not?

- What is your favorite way to move?

- How can you challenge yourself not only physically but emotionally to move forward?

- Close your eyes and imagine yourself in the words of Hebrews 12:1-4. What does this look like for you? What are you throwing off and what are you running toward?

6: PRETTY LIES
Truth and Vulnerability

What if we practiced courage every single day?
~Kelly Rae Roberts

An assortment of blankets lay strewn around the living room. Errant Cheerios litter the floor and nestle in couch corners and abandoned half-drunk sippy cups leak milk on the rug. Three sets of pajamas and at least two pair of shoes lie haphazardly thrown; at least one toilet remains clogged with far too much toilet paper; and I lie motionless on the couch. A silent tear rolls down my cheek. Made for more? My mind wanders swiftly to a different life, a far different reality residing somewhere outside my toy, blanket and pillow fort, Cheerio consumed house.

For as long as I can remember I have ached to be a mom. As a young girl I would take visiting babies out to the swing in my backyard and sit for hours, secretly hoping their mothers would forget them or leave them in my care. What possibly could there be in this world to do other than love them? What more could there be to life than to hold them, kiss them, rock them, sing lullabies to them? And then I grew up and became a mother. I quickly realized how much more there is to do. The lies come so easily.

I go down quickly. A single silent tear quickly snowballs into that wracking, sobbing mess of fear that I'm a terrible wife, the worst possible mother to even consider (let alone admit) that at times I don't want to be home with my children. I become convinced I am a pathetic wreck of a friend who sometimes doesn't know if she has another true friend in the world. I'm alone. In the frightening momentary reality of the lies in my head it is true. Painfully, jarringly, heart-wrenchingly true.

I was made for more than this! I have dreams! I want to be somebody! Surely the daily drudgery of motherhood laundry, vacuuming, mopping, cleaning, bill paying, potty training, and bottom wiping . . . there has to be more, right?!

It's in moments like these, when we're overwhelmed with our circumstances and underwhelmed with ourselves, that we start telling ourselves the lies that we're not enough—that we're somehow missing out on something else, something more. We wonder if we're less capable, successful, or relevant than our working female friends. And it's a steep, slippery slope.

The same is true for mothers who work outside the home. Whether they choose to pursue a career or must out of necessity, they face a similar guilt and pack of lies. Wondering if they made the right choice, they worry they're missing out by not being home every day with their kids or if they're somehow inferior or less maternal than their stay-at-home mom friends.

All of it is lies, bred out of the inferiority and insecurity that rests in our humanity. Though a part of us knows the truth even at the time, the lies still seem so real. In the moment it feels absolutely unbearable; doesn't it?

So much time can be wasted in the battlefield of the mind. The raging war of our gods as we try desperately to please others, strive for perfection, and suppress our truth for someone else's comfort or ease. But it's never for their benefit in the end because untruth builds bigger barriers, walls, resentments, wounds, and brokenness than existed in the first place. If we were just honest in the beginning, truthful in the end, we could spare ourselves so much time, energy, and heartache.

When we live to please others we fail ourselves. We fail those we love the most. When we surrender to our gods we fail the God that lives in us. Today is the day we start practicing courage. Today is the day we go to war with our gods and fight with everything we have to find truth.

TRUTH AND VULNERABILITY

So what is truth? Merriam-Webster defines it as 1. Sincerity in action, character and utterance; 2. Fact or actuality; judgment, proposition or idea that is true or accepted as true; or 3. A statement in accord with fact or actuality.[12]

In the case of relationship, there can be many truths; right? Have you ever been in a standoff with someone over truth? Good Lord, take a seat. We'll get to more of that later.

If we don't first seek His truth, how can we profess to know it? If we're not truthful with ourselves, how can we be honest with others? How can we live transparently, wholeheartedly alive, and awake if we're living for someone or something else first? If God, our husbands, our children, and ourselves are second, third, or somewhere farther down the ladder, if we endlessly search for someone else to blame, never taking responsibility for our own words, choices and actions, how can we even hope to grow?

Truth is always found in the open, by way of the light. Living in the open is scary because it requires vulnerability. Nakedness. It requires us to say yes to light, love, truth, honesty, forgiveness, openness, and wholeness. It requires us to lay down our deeply entrenched beliefs that perception is reality and find the courage to be who we are with our whole hearts. It means understanding that what we look for in others is the ability for them to be authentic and vulnerable with us—the same things we try to hide or suppress in ourselves.

I want you to have the courage to say yes to the spirit within you that so desperately wants to be loved and enough and realize that you already are loved and enough. "It's the brave who say a prayerful yes, the brave and wise who believe that the faith-filled yes is what heals things."[13]

And maybe it's as simple as that: choosing yes, saying yes, believing yes, every day when the difficult moment comes. Say yes to truth, life, love, grace, peace, and joy. Say no to jealousy, competition, critical spirits, dissension, and division. Proclaim a prayerful yes to all that is good and a firm no to all that destroys. Over time and practice, this courage becomes real; it becomes our authentic self. And we begin to speak truth and live truth and be our truth, wholly authentic, alive and free.

It's the wise who find their identity in Christ. In the perfect masterpiece created when He made you wholly and dearly loved, adored, relentlessly pursued, and yet free. We are free to choose whether we will follow Him, read His word, and listen to His teaching. How much more does He long for us? We search in vain, hiding and fumbling in the dark, and all the while our fullness is waiting patiently by our side—waiting for the choosing, for us to say yes.

So it's the choosing then that's the hardest part. Choosing yes means we let go of our false sense of control. It means we open our hands and begin to have faith. It's what makes our hearts flutter and our knees go weak. The giving up of our desire for concrete answers or carefully crafted plans, in exchange for cultivating our faith, is the belief in something for which there is no proof.

When our selfish hearts want nothing more than to say no to what we know will offer grace, love, gentleness, and peace, that is the precise moment we must practice courage. That is when we step out in faith and say yes—yes to light, yes to healing, yes to grace, yes to us and to who we are in this very moment. It's one of the bravest things we do.

AM I LIVING A REAL OR PRETEND REALITY?

Growing up, my mother always taught me there were two kinds of people: real people and pretend people.

Being a person who finds it difficult if not impossible to pretend things are okay when they're not, I could never understand how some people could act as though life wasn't hard. People whom I knew faced horrible tragedy in their personal lives, people who shared a desperate heartache raging inside the confines of their soul, were somehow able to walk out the door and put on a smiling face.

There are people you encounter who, if you didn't know what was happening behind closed doors, you'd never guess in a million years are carrying great burdens. Some of these people are fiercely strong. A small number of them wage battles you and I will never know with the grace, dignity, and faith that could move mountains. They share their battles with trusted friends; people who have earned the right to know their story and help shoulder the weight of their pain.

Their smile isn't the smile of a suffocated pain but of a smoldering hope, cradled in the protective arms of a few who are trusted—the few who have earned the title of true friend. For these, sadness and pain is temporary because of the community of grace and love that surrounds them. For these lucky ones, they just need time. These are the people who have become *real*.

Far too many of the rest are pretending. You, me, the girl next door, the neighbor down the street—the ones who you think have it all together, the one with the elusive perfect life—we all are pretenders. We're afraid to be real because living in our reality is hard. We've got real problems and real pain and numbing just seems so much easier.

Accepting our reality, and living in that reality, requires hard work and extraordinary courage because reality requires us to change. Reality requires us to evaluate the ways we live, what we can learn from our past, and how we must grow to find peace.

Pretend people have fallen for the lie that brokenness means weakness. After all, weakness is what they see with the naked eye. All that matters is what appears to be true, not what really is true. But what lies beneath the surface of a truly broken spirit is a deliberately surrendered strength—a strength that grows steady in the shadow of humility. What you find when you go deeper is a fortitude that becomes uncompromising in the light of truth. You discover a strength whose very nature illuminates the power of a supernatural God. There are two steps to becoming real. One: stop pretending. Two: give grace.

STOP PRETENDING

It's no big shock that we're all experts at living superficial lives. The bigger challenge is admitting it and boldly stepping free from it.

Pretending we're not hurting or grieving, that we're not struggling, suffocating, and drowning doesn't help us find solid ground. It keeps us wanting. It keeps us searching in darkness, fumbling around like a blind man with a candle in our hand when all we need to do is light the match.

What we've been doing isn't working. This game? This crazy, superficial, self-centered, fantasy isn't working. The definition of insanity is doing the same thing over and over again and expecting a different result. Change!

You must decide over and over again to stop pretending. You must find safe people with whom you can be vulnerable. Surround yourself with people who allow and encourage you to speak your truth, honor your feelings, express your pain, and imperfectly progress to the woman you desire to be—the woman God made you to be. The more time you spend with real people the less you'll be drawn to the pretend kind.

Our bodies are made to crave. Every Christmas season I start craving chocolate and sweets. I don't know what it is; but, the more I eat, the more I want. The same is true of our souls. The more we engage with true, honest, authentic, and real people, the more we crave it. And the more we surround ourselves with the real stuff, the more we become aware of, and the less we desire the counterfeit.

Step up, stand up, show up. It's time to get real.

AM I TELLING MYSELF THE TRUTH?

Jeremiah tells us the heart is deceitful above all things. (see Jeremiah 17:9) What is truth and how can we know if we're telling ourselves the truth if our hearts are deceitful above all things?

The unfortunate reality of lying to ourselves is that we get really good at it. In fact, by adulthood we're pretty much experts. Quite often we can't differentiate the lies from the truth. We're embroiled in patterns that go back to our childhood when we made agreements with ourselves about who we are. Perhaps we didn't feel loved by a parent or felt invisible to a group of friends or peers. Chances are we accepted a lie that we weren't good enough or loveable enough to deserve their attention or affection, and that lie has woven itself into the fabric of our adult lives. As it resurfaces throughout our lives, we go back to that original belief structure and wrongly reaffirm it as true.

It's a vicious cycle and one very difficult to break. Even though we may consciously know these agreements are a lie, they are hard to overwrite even with diligent effort and repetition. After all, we've staked so much of our identity on them. The lies are as much a part of us as the truth: our deeply known worthiness. Because at the core of our spirit is a knowledge that we are created wholly and deeply loved. (see Colossians 3:12)

The frightening reality of being wholly and deeply loved by others means we have to be wholly and deeply KNOWN. And being known requires vulnerability. It requires us to tear down the walls we've built believing they would keep us safe, removing the masks, and risking rejection to find authentic community. To find our people—the ones who will love us, accept us, see us, and know us, the ones who will stand by us and with us, who will fight for us—is the hard work; it's our life work.

MIRROR, MIRROR ON THE WALL

How many times do you look at yourself in the mirror each day? If you're like me, sometimes you steal a glance in the mirror and scare yourself! Many nights I apply a salicylic acid treatment to spots all over my face. Whether they really need it or not, I think it helps and I dab it on. My husband smiles as he climbs into bed, shaking his head, saying, "Goodnight, Pocahontas." Needless to say, there have been a few times I forgot to look at myself before leaving the house and later caught a glimpse of myself with slightly sleep-faded pink streaks covering my entire face. The Pocahontas look isn't quite as endearing the next morning at preschool dropoff!

Although the desire of my heart for this book is to get you away from the mirror, and away from your external appearance, for right now, I am urging you to head to the nearest mirror. Or, better yet, find one where you can have a few minutes alone.

Are you there yet? Take a moment and just look at the beautiful face looking back at you. Don't say or do anything quite yet; just look. Look into your eyes; see the small freckle on the side of your cheek or the dimple in your heart shaped chin or the way your hair curls just around your temple. You are beautiful. You really are.

What are the agreements you made about yourself when you were young? What lies have you lived with for so many years that you believe are true? Who hurt you? Is there a pattern you see repeating over and over in your life? What is it? Who or what do you find at the center of your pain?

Whatever heartache is burning inside you right now, feel it. Let it come to the forefront of your mind. Look into your eyes as the feelings of hurt, pain, grief, longing, rejection, and abandonment well up. Don't look away.

Now, let her talk. That's right, you. Talk. Out loud. Keep looking at your face in the mirror. Speak your heart, your truth, the truthiest truth you know, and don't look away. Every time you're tempted to look away, ask yourself why. I've discovered it's infinitely harder to lie to myself when I'm looking in the mirror and talking out loud. I can sense my own deceit—my own desire to sway the story my way or to convince myself of a truth that isn't really real. Look at her. Look at you. Don't lie to yourself anymore. The game begins and ends with you. This is your moment.

Tell yourself the truth, not what you feel, because feelings are fickle, changing from day to day, moment to moment. Tell yourself the truth. Why are you angry? Why are you hurt? Who let you down? What makes you afraid? You'll be surprised what's hiding in the darkness, trapped just beneath the surface. Things you don't even know about yourself will rise to the top and have the chance for healing if you don't look away.

In order to find love, you have to first love yourself. In order to love yourself, you have to know yourself. Let yourself be seen, known, cared for, and truly loved by you. I know to some of you this might seem weird or crazy (or both), but the truth remains: if you're not honest with yourself, you will never be free. Give yourself the gift of freedom. You were made to be free. And when you feel afraid—and you will—think of my beautiful tree.

I have this tree in my yard that sits just outside my window, and in the fall it turns the most striking scarlet red. One fall day I was looking out the window admiring her beauty. In a sudden rush I watched as the thoughtless wind ripped nearly every beautiful scarlet leaf from her branches and carried them away. Placing my hand over my mouth I saw her for what she now was: naked. Exposed. Vulnerable.

It got me thinking how often I feel like my tree. The seasons of life allow me to change my leaves, present to the world the way I choose to show my best self. Some days I wear my fancy leaves, some days I wear my comfy leaves, and some days I just feel ugly. I am nothing but branches; nothing fits. I've got "nothing to wear," and everything I put on just seems wrong. I feel fake. I'm trying too hard, so I put my sweats back on and forget about it.

But why does a tree lose her leaves for winter? Much like a plant you cut back in the fall, it's to conserve energy, to push strength to her roots so she can survive the harsh conditions. Realizing this, I started to feel more like my beautiful naked tree. There are times in my life when I'm not wearing my pretty leaves. I'm more exposed, more vulnerable to those around me. I share my heart, my life, hopes, dreams, disappointments, and failures. I take risks; I dare to be bold. Authentic. Brave.

Sometimes in the midst of these bouts of bravery I am tempted to shrink, to put my leaves back on. But I remember my tree that sheds her leaves and boldly exposes her vulnerability to the harsh and violent conditions so she may be strengthened from within, so her energy is focused on that which is essential to survive. She is deepening and strengthening her roots so she can be stronger and healthier, and in the spring she can sprout new growth.

I look at my tree in a new way; her bare branches now speak inexpressible beauty. They proclaim a freedom to be bold, to be brave in harsh weather, to have faith in the rhythm of nature and the constitution of our faith that all things work together for our refinement.

This life is about being brave. So often I am tempted to put my leaves back on and just be pretty. But you know what? Pretty doesn't cut it anymore.

TELLING OTHERS THE TRUTH

I'm a big fan of overlooking an offense. If it's minor or unintended and doesn't affect the foundation of the relationship, then it's best to just let it go. *Que sera sera.* But there are times and circumstances where you must be honest, when you must practice courage, take a big, deep breath, and tell the truth to someone else.

The rule I follow is simple: if it would be more detrimental to the relationship to remain quiet, then I tell the truth. Ways that it could be more detrimental include things such as requiring me to lie; changing or deteriorating the security or trust in the relationship by keeping quiet; and creating or fostering resentment, insecurity, or jealousy.

Stripping your pride and humbly telling someone you are hurt is actually braver than remaining silent. It requires vulnerability. It's an act of bravery to open your heart to someone who has already hurt you and allow them even deeper access. You expose an already troubled heart to their response. It can go one of two ways, but I see it as a very personal invitation. If you didn't truly care about the person, you would let it go. If it hurts enough to lovingly address it, it allows the opportunity for the friendship to go deeper and wider.

We each bear scars from our pasts and they aren't the responsibility of everyone we meet. But in the process of authentic relationship, we have the opportunity to understand each other, wounds and all. We get to know painful triggers and how to avoid them. We get to learn how to help each other instead of cause further harm. This is not so we enable bad or unhealthy behavior, but so we learn to love others well. We learn to see beyond ourselves, beyond our annoyance or pride, and see the heart of a friend—the true, tender heart of a woman who desires to be seen and known, loved, cared for, and accepted in spite of (and because of) her faults.

With skin in the game and flesh on the line, real friendships go deep. They risk and they dare; they dream and they live. They stand by and they wait; they nurture and they love. In life and in love, how deep do you go?

For most of us, we're just skimming the surface of a superficial life. Desperate to be known but afraid of deep water. We long for it, and yet it is our biggest fear. But this life is about freedom; we were made to be free.

GIVE GRACE

Speaking our truth to friends or others in relationship does not give us license to spew anger and frustration all over them. Just because we believe something is true doesn't mean it is. Remember that the heart is deceitful above all things. We can be totally out of line, completely misunderstand a comment or situation, and firmly believe that we are right and wrongly believe we are the authors of truth. It just isn't so.

If you cannot approach a friend or acquaintance in a loving, grace-filled manner, then you are not the one to speak truth. You are not ready to express and expose your heart because it's not about your heart yet. If you're angry, vengeful, or only seeking to blame someone else then it's not about truth at all, it's about being right. There are many different truths in any one situation and if your desire is to sway someone to your position or get them to give in to your truth, then you'd best find a quiet place and pull out your mirror again. Figure out why you're so angry and why you so desperately want to be right. Determine why you cannot move on and out of bitterness.

Proverbs tells us that "wounds from a friend can be trusted." (Proverbs 27:6) A true friend is willing to say something that might cause a temporary hurt in order to save us from something harder or more painful down the road. A true friend says the hard things, she sees us sometimes better than we see ourselves, and she cares enough to save us from our sin. If you've been hurt by a friend, think back to whether they were trustworthy and if what they said was truth. If you've written them off out of pride or anger, when deep down you know they meant only the best for you, seek reconciliation. True friends are hard to find and it's worth keeping every one you've got.

GATHERING LEAVES

I think of truth-telling like gathering leaves. Like our truth, every leaf is different; no two are the same. So often we gather them, every leaf to build our case. Stacking them upon one another—higher, higher, higher. Which pile will reach the sky? Surely my truth will prevail. But a sudden wind blows. Her delicate breath sends a ripple through the leaves. The gatherers rush to save their high towers, but who can stop the wind? First a whisper, and then a gust and the leaves are scattered. So too, is the relationship.

How much better would it be to gather them together? One pile, built by two. Each leaf is gathered with thoughtful care, a sincere heart, humble spirit, and a gentle hand. Done with care, you see each other's truth, you see the simple error or misunderstanding, and are left with a heaping pile, perfect, for jumping! This is an exercise growing and strengthening the bond of a true, deep, enduring friendship. Together, you discover the remarkable padding that belies the hard ground underneath. Rolling to your backs, you stare at the sky, contemplating the vastness of life and the smallness of struggle.

Sometimes truth hurts. It's uncomfortable. No one likes to hear a hard truth. But wounds from a friend can be trusted. Truth heals. We can deal with truth. We can work with truth. Silence, bitterness, and unforgiveness are dead end roads. Even if truth brings anger or disappointment, hurt or disrespect, when we speak truth in love it gets it outside of us where roots of unspoken bitterness lose their ability to silently poison us from the inside. It allows the opportunity for understanding— not agreement, but understanding. Resolution of a matter does not require one party to acquiesce to another's truth. That wouldn't be sincere and could never be truth.

Truth allows the opportunity for the myriad of tiny ways we can begin the process of dialogue, counsel, forgiveness, restoration, healing, and grace. All relationship will have struggle and disagreement or it's just not real. And true friendship is padding for our fall—individual leaves, unique truths, gathered together to buffer the sting.

The next time you're preparing to tell some truth or work through a conflict or difficult situation, remember the leaves. Gather them together. Be careful of the wind. And I pray it will prove to be a soft place to land.

REFLECTION

- Do you consider yourself a real or pretend person?

- Is there a lie you keep telling yourself or believing about yourself?

- What are you getting from that lie? Attention, compassion, time? In order for us to continue a behavior that is destructive to ourselves, we must be getting something from it. What is the benefit for you? Is it worth it?

- Complete the exercise in this chapter looking in the mirror. What rose to the surface? What is one step you will commit to taking to heal that wound?

- Have you ever felt exposed and naked like my beautiful tree? What did the experience teach you?

- How can you begin to practice telling the truth to yourself and others?

PART THREE
LOOKING OUT

7: PRETTY CRITICAL
It's Not About You

We have the opportunity to learn from life or ignore its teaching.
~Nicole Johnson

I'm sure you've had your fair share of critics. The voices that try to keep you from following your dream, using your voice, creating your art, or shining your light. Sometimes we call them mom, dad, brother, sister, or friend. And, we'll get to them, but chances are there's a bigger, louder voice that tears down your dream, criticizes your efforts and tries to get you to quit. Do you have one of those critics? Me too. It's me. And I bet it's you, too.

I've struggled in female relationships for as long as I can remember. It's not this way with all of them, but a pattern of difficult female relationships has woven a steady thread through the tapestry of my life. From the time I was a very young girl I believed I wasn't enough. I wasn't interesting enough, smart enough, athletic enough, or valuable enough to the people I loved the most.

We've all been there. This isn't a personal attack on my family or the friends I had growing up. I watch it going on right now in my own little family. Sibling rivalry, conflicting demands, the competitive dance for attention and sheer exhaustion all add to the chaos and dysfunction we call family. I think back to how I felt as a child and sometimes I see my own face reflected back in the faces of my children and it breaks my heart. We're human. We can and do fail.

Experiences in my most vital relationships as a child, in combination with the difficult ones with girls in adolescence, contributed to the blaring voice in my head that would often tell me I wasn't worthy of female relationship. The message that something was intrinsically wrong with me was on replay—a pattern doomed to repeat itself.

Though I knew in my head this was the furthest thing from the truth, sometimes our hearts don't get the message. It is a wrongly rooted belief that still makes me uneasy around certain women who share similar characteristics to these women in my past—women I love, whom I still care for deeply, but who have hurt me.

A LONG, DARK DRIVEWAY

My mom gave me permission to share this story, though it will still be difficult for her to read it here. I know my mom loves me, and always has, but sometimes the most primary relationships are the ones that hurt us the most. Though they may not mean to cause pain, they have their own story from a time long past that they've pushed away but still carry alongside them.

My parents had a rocky marriage for much of my childhood. When it was good, it was good, but it was a difficult relationship. When I was thirteen my mom left my dad for a short time and moved in with my grandma. She took me with her. One night, after taking a bath, I came into the kitchen to hear my grandma speaking poorly about my dad. Standing in the middle of the kitchen covered only in my bath towel, I defended my dad with every fighting word a little girl knows. I told my grandma to go to hell.

She didn't take it well. She had me pack my bags and kicked me out of her house. I was told to call my dad to pick me up and to wait outside until he came. Home was about an hour and a half away. Standing by the garage I began to change out of my towel when my grandma came out of the house and marched her stout, grumpy legs toward me. She stopped mid-driveway, pointed her finger down the gravel road and said, "You will wait at the end of the driveway. I don't want you near this house."

The driveway was about a quarter mile long and sat on a busy two-lane highway that connected Minneapolis to northern Wisconsin. In my little bare feet, I walked the agate-strewn driveway, flanked on either side by large cornfields. It was already getting dark, and I was scared of the dark.

With my towel and my little bag I sat down by the side of the driveway. I don't remember what I did during those ninety minutes. My only memory was looking back at the old farmhouse, lit up like a Christmas tree in the dark of the night. I saw my mom sitting at the kitchen table with my grandma and I wondered if she saw me. I wondered if they even cared if I was okay.

My mom and I never spoke about what happened at grandma's house. That is, until at thirty-five years old, when I became aware of the foundation it laid for the voice of my inner critic. How, because of that initial experience, I had continued to perpetuate a life-long story of unworthiness. Alone on that driveway, I resigned myself to the belief that I was unworthy of love from two of the women who should've loved me the most—women who should have fought for me, accepted me, and protected me, but didn't.

I forgive my mom and grandma for what happened that night a long time ago. She and my dad were struggling, and there was much going on in the depths of her own soul. But the story is still mine, and it matters. It shaped a large part of who I am, what I believed, and how I lived. And it rooted in me the strength to overcome.

As painful as it was, and as terrible as it might sound, I wouldn't change it. I wouldn't take it back. I love my mother for reasons unrelated to what she can do for me. I love her because she is mine. And the truth is, as a parent, every single one of us has left our child sitting at the end of the driveway in one way or another. But the mother-daughter relationship is unlike any other. Fraught with failure, disappointment, and unrelenting, uncompromising love, it is one of the fiercest relationships of all. I have yet to meet a friend who doesn't have a piece of her heart broken by her own mother, and yet continues to love her in the very deepest places of her soul.

We all have a story, and we all have pain. Messy and broken and threadbare and full; we stand in the midst of our lives. And we allow a God who is able to fill in the space where man has failed us, to cover over what causes us pain, and to heal where we are so badly broken. We listen for His voice to record over the agreements we made as a child about who we were, who and what we were worthy of, and what we deserved.

A TATTERED TAPESTRY

When I say the words *mother, father, brother, sister*, they evoke emotion. They are not neutral words. There is story indelibly and intrinsically linked to these words. And there is pain. There is brokenness and rejection and abandonment and wounds that we've never dealt with and, therefore, have never healed.

We may say we don't care and we insist that we're fine; meanwhile we're dying inside from wounds we don't even know it because we've never uncovered the source. We've never wanted to feel the pain and so we've stuffed it away, excused it, convinced ourselves it's fine. We're fine. But we carry it with us.

We find people to repeat the story because when we were young and weren't old enough to understand, we decided it was about us. We determined we weren't good enough, smart enough, pretty enough, funny enough, or worthy enough, and we believed it. And when it happened again with someone else it confirmed that belief. It rooted in us more deeply. And so we looked for people throughout our lives to recreate the scenario, and desperately fought for a different ending. And we failed again and again because it was never about us in the first place

REARVIEW MIRROR

We all have critics and most often we're our very loudest and harshest one. From where does your harshness come? What happened to you when you were young? When did you make an agreement with yourself that you were unworthy, unlovable, ugly, or stupid? What made you feel you had to live your life to please someone else?

We have all made decisions about ourselves and our worthiness when we were too young or had faulty or incomplete information. We've all made these agreements. The challenge is figuring out when and why. Take back your power to rewrite the story through the eyes of an adult. Know that very little that happens to us in this life is our fault. The way people treat us is, in most cases, a reflection of how they feel about themselves. It is a reaction to what happened to them in their own lives. We just happen to be in the wrong place at the wrong time. The way in which we judge and criticize others is a direct reflection of the way we feel most vulnerable or insecure in our own lives.

For most of us, we look back on our lives and wonder why things happened to us the way they did and why we had to suffer the experiences and pain we went through. We look back in the rearview mirror of *what happened to us.* I challenge you to turn the car around and drive headfirst into your past. Turn on the brights and see it from the new perspective of *what was given to us.*

Each of us is given a story—some much harder, darker, and more painful than others—but we all have pain. We all suffer loss, tragedy, heartache, and despair. We all had unfortunate things happen to us when we were young. But our story is our testimony. It is the light that we bear in a life full to the brim of pain. The gift we share with others who come up behind us with a similarly shattered life. We get the privilege of understanding. Blessed with compassion, grace, and mercy we are invited to participate in the miracle of healing. We get to be teachers, lovers, encouragers, caregivers, and friends all because we were given a story and we had the courage to turn around and face it—to learn from it and change what we believed.

REFLECTION

- Look into the rearview mirror of your life. Do you see patterns of painful relationships or situations? How does it make you feel?

- Can you think back to the first time you felt that feeling? How has that feeling stopped you from living the life you desire?

- How can you now, as an adult, reframe what happened to you or see how it was not about you or your fault?

- Is there any way you can see what happened to you as a gift? Maybe it is not the one you wanted or would've chosen for your life, but can you still see it is a gift? What beautiful thing was borne through that hardship that otherwise never would've been?

8: PRETTY MEAN
Jealousy, Insecurity, and Toxic Friendships

Anger is cruel and fury overwhelming,
but who can stand before jealousy?
~Proverbs 27:4

S tomping the dirt off my shoes, I bring noise into the quiet stillness of the room. She's standing there, looking right at me, but she doesn't notice me. She looks right past me . . . through me, really. Her eyes glaze and slowly shift to the realm outside the door I just walked through, the door right behind my back. She noticed me. Didn't she? Clearly she saw me, but doesn't want me to know. She doesn't want to convey her own weary heart, the one being silently poisoned by the bitterness waging a desperate war inside her spirit. She needs to escape, to flee from what this room now holds: me.

She maneuvers around me without looking at me, talking to me, or touching me as if proximity to me is some kind of death to her. It's as if my presence might somehow contradict the truth warring in her mind—a battle already well settled and scored. I sense an angst rising in her spirit, for which her only remedy is escape. She edges around me, silent, robotic, opens the door, and is gone. A quick chill punches through the room as the door quietly shuts. Not a word. Not a glance. Nothing. I turn to see her walk away. She doesn't look back.

I walk past her weeks later, and again, months later. She still doesn't see me. I look around, down at my body, to others in the room. *I am here, right?* I silently ask myself.

Have you ever felt invisible? Ignored, left out, or overlooked as if your presence had no value? Perhaps indifferent is the worst response of them all. It silently, but effectively, communicates: *You don't matter one way or the other, because I have no feeling for you at all.*

It's unsettling, isn't it? I'm sure you've felt it too. It's the human experience and, more specifically, the female experience. It started very early in my young life and starts even earlier for girls now. Young girls in the first grade begin practicing their strategy in the games of inclusion, popularity, and the competitive dance for worthiness, belonging, and value.

Who will be the leader? Who will fall in line? We find mean girls in the making and beautiful hearts sitting on the bench or stuck watching from the sidelines.

We women are an interesting lot. Nurturing and soft, tender and loving and yet we have the capacity to be cruel, exclusive, competitive, and hurtful. We've all been there. Chances are, each of us has taken our turn in both roles: the mean girl and the one in the crosshairs. But, why?

What compels women to take an ounce of joy out of thrashing another woman? Cutting her down to her face or behind her back, it doesn't matter; it's just as vicious either way. As a woman I have a difficult time understanding it, I can only imagine how confusing and annoying it is for our male counterparts. Our husbands and partners, who by nature glide over trivial misunderstandings, suffer with us through the ongoing drama in female relationships. No matter our age, mean girls are a common thread in our lives.

I remember in the sixth grade I took my turn in a common game some girls still play—the awful one where every girl was turned against me. Not one was allowed to openly play with or talk to me for an entire week. Of course I had a few secret friends, but they couldn't openly let on they liked me in public or they would find themselves next in line. I would go to school, sit by myself, be by myself, walk the playground at recess by myself. I was left to wonder, hide, and cry by myself. That is, until a kind and brave teacher had the compassion to notice. With a peacemaker's heart she told those girls, without mincing words, what she thought of their behavior and that it would end that day.

It's tempting to trivialize experiences such as this. After all, it's a part of growing up. We all know that middle school is one of the most difficult times in a young girl's life. I've met countless girls and women who share a similar story to mine. But trivializing it doesn't change the impact such a story has on our lives. It doesn't erase the pain or humiliation or give back the self-confidence and trust that it stole from us. Regardless of its significance or triviality, it shapes us. Mine is not a tragic story; it's the human story. And more specifically, it's the female story.

This is a story that has informed each of the female relationships I've had in my life ever since. It is a seemingly innocuous schoolyard game that leaves unseen scars on a young girl's heart: fear, mistrust, rejection, and humiliation. I've lived it long enough that it's become a second skin, the layer under the more beautiful one of thriving and rich female relationships. Scratch the surface and it's there. Fear, shame, rejection, insecurity, and brokenness reside in that subdermal layer. But just as brutal as the rocky path of women relationships has been, I've been blessed with a multitude of very deep, meaningful, life-giving relationships with women all along the way. I think it's the story God had for my life. The story He wanted me to know. The story He now wants me to tell.

If we're not mindful, some of the cruel behaviors learned in middle school can carry over into our adult lives. Things like jealousy and gossip are so woven into our sinful nature that if we're not fighting it, we're doing it. Have you ever experienced the harshness or cruelty of another woman? From a stranger, an acquaintance, a friend even? Her cold snub or jarring comment left you in bewilderment wondering, *What in the world just happened?* Did it leave you to simmer in the meaning of her abrasive words or silent anger for days, weeks, or months? Did you feel the chill from a group as one girl spread her invisible poison amongst them, slowly, but decisively edging you out?

Perhaps it was the mean girls' playground of your middle school years. Maybe it was the competition and ranking for position with the high school boys and invitations to parties, sports, and music productions, or grades and college admissions. It could have been the adult women who failed to grow beyond the petty games of the schoolyard. Regardless of the details of your broken story, there is health and healing to be found in the journey.

THE GAME: TOXIC FRIENDSHIPS

Sometimes we play games in our heads; but, in this game, we're the only player. We put on our narcissist hat and think everything and everyone revolves around us. Every look, smirk, joke, or whisper we observe, we think it's about us. *The girl laughing over there? She's laughing at me. The two telling secrets? Yup, about me. The group of girls who just walked by without saying hello, or even returning a glance . . . deliberate. That comment on Facebook? Me again.*

Sometimes the game wins. Self-centeredness, bitterness, jealousy, envy, pride, and greed serve as silent killers. They take root and choke the life out of us. They steal all that is good and cover everything real. Sometimes we're the player; sometimes we're the mark.

THE PLAYER

If we're playing and we've got enough quarters, we can entertain ourselves to delirium. We can create elaborate delusive experiences in our minds, planting seeds of doubt, envy, and malice in the fertile soil of our hearts. We nurture these seedlings until they are thick trunks of bitterness with deep expansive roots—the very essence of the plant choking out the oxygen of life.

The small talk that grew into gossip, the persuasion or manipulation that led to a lie, these innocent activities subtly become something more toxic. Once quiet insecurities transform into festering jealousies, critical spirits, and judgment of others. Sin brings death. Always.

The seeds of bitterness, jealousy, and envy will always result in death of friendship, relationship, and self because a bitter heart creates a closed off, walled up, scared to touch, choking to death, life.

WOMEN & JEALOUSY

Why are some girls mean? Why do some mean girls never grow out of it? I can't pretend to know all the answers; but, through experience, I have discovered that the greatest bitter root that lies in the soil of a mean girl's heart is jealousy. It thrives on feelings of insecurity, fear, and anxiety over the loss of something she values.

Jealousy is real and ever watchful. Prone to vain imaginations, it presents itself with emotions of anger, resentment, inadequacy, helplessness, and disgust. Only the keeper of this beast can battle against it, and even then the battle remains. Only God can pour forth what is needed to uproot and destroy this bitter root. Unchecked, jealousy will destroy everything in her life.

If you struggle with jealousy you must make a choice every day, every moment, not to go there. Decide that you won't let fear and insecurity control you and strangle the life from your relationships. Stop the wandering thoughts that lead only to destruction. We must all choose to live in the uncomfortable reality that the world, and everyone in it, does not revolve around us. Not every perceived slight is about us. You must put your identity, security, and trust in God, not in the flawed perception that you have control.

Relinquishing control over jealousy is a difficult and intentional process because the very mechanism of jealousy desires to control physically what it cannot control emotionally. Jealousy's fits of rage and bitter, angry words are the ways it attempts to control a person or situation. It will always fail. Jealousy will devour and destroy every single relationship you have, *if* you let it.

THE MARK

If you've been the mark of jealousy you must be strong enough to let go. Healthy relationships are made of healthy people who set and hold healthy boundaries. There are many forms of healthy relationship. If you're in one, you usually know. It feels good! Though no perfect relationship exists, a healthy friendship is covered with an overall feeling of calm and peace. Common threads of healthy relationships include: freedom, grace, forgiveness, honest and open communication, and choosing the best of, and for, one another.

HEALTHY RELATIONSHIPS

For me, personal freedom is a foundational cornerstone of a healthy friendship. Relationships must be free if we're going to grow! Some people don't want relationships to change; these friends want things to always remain as they are or have always been. Though there is comfort in consistency, these friendships operate under a false sense of security. Life is a never-ending process of learning. If we are truly committed to learning, by necessity we must grow and change. If one friend desires to learn and grow and one friend wants everything to stay the same, there will be tension. Healthy relationships allow freedom to grow and change over time.

Not all friendships are made to be life-long. Some of my seasonal friendships have taught me the most about myself!

Some of the relationships I've lost or let go have been the catalyst for my greatest strides toward maturity. Just because a friendship comes to a close, or parts for a time, it doesn't mean this person wasn't a valuable friend. It doesn't mean there wasn't a lesson to be learned or that the relationship was a failure. Each friendship, whether a season or a lifetime, offers value and purpose to our journey.

Healthy relationships reveal the best in both parties. If one friend makes a comment that can be taken two different ways, a healthy friend chooses to believe the better alternative. And if they are unsure, they have the courage to ask! A healthy friend will seek clarity to keep the relationship strong and secure and not let doubt, fear, or insecurity get a foothold. Healthy people trust that they can have open and honest communication with one another.

Finally, healthy relationships offer grace and forgiveness. We are going to bump up against each other in life. We're going to say things we don't mean, and we're going to be sorry we said some things we did mean! We have to be big enough people that we can offer grace and forgiveness in the same way we need it from others. This life is hard, and so often we make it so much harder with bitter hearts and unforgiving spirits. We've got to allow ourselves to be free to be imperfect, and we've got to let others be free and imperfect too.

UNHEALTHY RELATIONSHIPS

Just as there are many types of healthy relationships, there are many variations of unhealthy ones as well. Much of it boils down to gut feelings—those illustrious "red flags." So often we fail to listen to our inner voices when they tells us to be cautious of a person. We tell ourselves we're being too hard on them, too judgmental, too critical and that we should give them the benefit of the doubt. And what happens? We ignore that voice, proceed without caution, and find ourselves down the road in some sort of mess. And we knew it from the start! Somehow, someway, we knew.

We need to stop pushing our conscience aside and consider it the wise voice of intuition. Your intuition is not comprised of random feelings. It is the voice of your life experience—the sum total of the circumstances, successes, and failures you have encountered and survived in your life. Your intuition is meant to guide you in your future. Bottom line: trust yourself. Don't give someone the benefit of the doubt over your own gut feeling. You know yourself and you're usually right about these things.

Some common signs of unhealthy relationship include: gossiping, pot-stirring, anger, bitterness, passive aggression, control, jealousy, and punishing behavior. If they talk to you *about* someone else, you can bet your life they will talk about you *to* someone else. You can write that one down with the Proverbs; that's just wisdom!

If a friend of yours is a constant gossip, beware. If they're always throwing off-hand or snide remarks to you or about others, trying to stir the pot between you and another person, or injecting jealousy into you when they're around, be watchful. These friends are prone to jealousy and they subconsciously want you to join them in their misery. Don't go there! Tread very carefully. Other unhealthy relationships can be rife with angry words, control, and punishment. If you somehow fail them or their expectations they let you know with silence, irritability, harsh words, or another form of punishment. It's not pretty.

Often we see the warning signs, but we stay close to our toxic friends because we're scared. We wrongly believe that staying in familiar unhealthy relationships is ultimately better than the unknown, or worse, being alone. Perhaps we're afraid if we let go it will reinforce the agreement we made that we're not worthy of relationship. We create vicious cycles of emotional turmoil when we allow fear to drive our decision-making. It's a problematic situation. When we stay close to toxic people, we keep healthy people away. And the chaos eats away the time we could be spending nurturing the positive, healthy, loving relationships in our lives.

It breaks my heart to meet a woman who has never had a safe friendship and doesn't know the gift of sharing life with a trusted, kindred spirit. In this kind of friendship there is freedom and grace to make mistakes, there is encouragement to dream, to grow, and to live with our whole hearts! It's a rare and beautiful thing.

If you're in an unhealthy relationship and find yourself the constant target of blame or anger, do your best to stay above the fray. Often these protracted disputes continue without your participation or cooperation. Most often, you've got to let go of the relationship to find emotional health. You must continually remind yourself you were called to be free, and, ultimately, it's not about you. Do not engage; these unhealthy disputes are often unnecessary and irrational, and they prolong an already painful process. Any engagement on your part will end up backfiring on you. Learn the signs of healthy and safe relationships and pursue them. Trust your instincts when you sense trouble, and slowly walk away. Beautiful friendships await you when you become healthy and move away from toxic people.

Don't let fear keep you from becoming whole and healthy. Don't allow a prior unhealthy or painful relationship hinder you from putting yourself out there or keep you from boldly stepping into the arena. You'll never find relationship unless you risk. And believe me, it's worth every bit of the risk to find a true friend. Be brave. Practice kindness. Cultivate compassion and forgiveness. Don't be quick to offense. Life is short and bitterness is rampant. You must stand apart. You must stand for something other than the status quo.

We are called to live at peace so long as it depends on us. (see Romans 12:18) Unfortunately, sometimes as far as it depends on us doesn't go far enough on it's own. Do you find yourself enmeshed in a toxic relationship where you cannot seem to make peace? Get out of the way. I can't promise very many things, but this one I can: you may be the target, but it's not about you. It was never about you.

If you're not careful you'll fall into the game. Slowly but surely, you'll start examining, inspecting, and investigating every detail. What you said, did, thought, meant, implied, and inferred—everything that could make you invisible, unknown, unwanted. But it was never about you. And now you're in, you're playing the game. Although it's tempting to try to figure it out, there is no good ending to this game. We've got to be full of something more than ourselves. Walk away. .

I say it as if it's easy. But I know it's not. My natural inclination is to endure, to wait it out. I tend to stand in the mud and slog through as if I could sift the dirt from water. It's an agonizing quagmire. The thought of walking away doesn't seem like the right thing to do. It seems easy, cheap. But the process proves arduous, with high costs on all sides.

PLANTING SEEDS

The garden is a wonderful metaphor for life. Seeds of life, grace, mercy, kindness, gentleness, and peace are always being planted in the soil of our hearts. Those seeds go on to produce fruit when we draw from the well and fill our bodies with living water. They yield friendship and relationship centered on and built in faith, moderated by grace and His truth, balanced by accountability and a forgiving spirit. As with any garden, there are seeds that don't belong. Seeds of gossip, doubt, dissension, bitterness, and envy are just as prevalent in the garden, and they grow like weeds. But we choose what we put into our bodies— the cup from which we will drink, the plants from which we will take shelter and grow.

In the parable of the seeds, Jesus tells a gathered crowd:

A farmer went out to sow his seed. As he was scattering the seed, some fell along the path; it was trampled on, and the birds of the air ate it up. Some fell on rock, and when it came up, the plants withered because they had no moisture. Other seed fell among thorns, which grew up with it and choked the plants. Still other seed fell on good soil. It came up and yielded a crop, a hundred times more than was sown." He said, "The seed is the word of God. Those along the path are the ones who hear, and then the devil comes and takes away the word from their hearts, so that they may not believe and be saved. Those on the rock are the ones who receive the word with joy when they hear it, but they have no root. They believe for a while, but in the time of testing they fall away. The seed that fell among thorns stands for those who hear, but as they go on their way they are choked by life's worries, riches and pleasures, and they do not mature. But the seed on good soil stands for those with a noble and good heart, who hear the word, retain it, and by persevering produce a crop.

—Luke 8:4-15

Jesus held relationship in high regard. He called us to relationship with one another—to sharpen, encourage, build character, and forgive, to gain wisdom, and speak truth in love. These friendships are rare and precious treasures. But some relationships corrupt good character.

Some may lead you to do things or participate in actions that go against your good judgment or moral fiber. They may be fraught with less obvious sin traps like gossip and judgment that breed a critical spirit. Or they may simply deteriorate in that murky swamp where your relationship merely subsists by sifting dirt from water. In this way, your relationship becomes a hindrance to your ongoing relationship with God. I've been in that place where my free time and thoughts were consumed by a stagnant relationship I would now characterize as thorns in the soil of my heart.

We are called to be kind and friendly to everyone, to do good to all people, especially those who belong to the family of believers. (see Galatians 6:10) But a righteous man is cautious in friendship. (see Proverbs 12:26) The human heart is not an easy field to cultivate. It's a land of hard, rocky, weedy soil. But one by one we must pull the weeds, cut away the thorns, and carry off the rocks that stand in the way of fertile soil.

In the wake of a rift or bitter division, I've been left so many times wondering if I am a bad person, or a bad friend. *Do some women hate me because of something I've done, or is it just who I am they seem to hate?* I've discovered those are very difficult questions because of the richness on the other side of the equation and the depth and breadth of meaningful female relationships that do not offer intimidation, competitiveness, or insecurity. Those are relationships where God is alive and present because He lives in each of us. This is where intimate thoughts, hopes, and dreams are shared in the space of safety, unconditional love, and positive regard. This is where I know I am deeply and fully loved. How do these two very distinct worlds coexist inside of and around me? I don't know. But they do. And I bet they do in you, too.

At the start of this chapter I told you that fear, shame, bitterness, and brokenness reside in my flesh, just beneath the surface of a put together life. And it's true. Scratch the surface and you'll find the scars. But slowly, over the last decade, the power of that sub-dermal layer is waning. Shame no longer holds a vice-like grip or I wouldn't be writing about it now. Of course it lurks. Shame always lurks, waiting for an opportunity to sprout a noxious weed. But when you're aware of your tendencies, when you know your weaknesses, you're better at tending the garden. You learn that it's best to pull the weeds before they take root, before they get in close and tangled in the plant.

It's not shameful to have a history of some difficult female relationships. They don't define us as much as the process that results because of them. These critical or tumultuous friendships, the immature ones of my youth and the conditional ones of my adulthood, have carved out a deeper well of compassion in me than ever could have existed without them. In some ways, they have made me stronger in myself.

This is not to point fingers at every girl who was ever mean to me or left me out of their group. It has to be deeper than that or I've learned nothing and am no better for the trial. What I'm here to testify is that, although it seems impossible, in the wake of rejection and cruelty I have begun to find my true identity in Christ, and I have come to know and like myself even more.

I am stronger, taller, braver. My faith has been renewed in the life-giving relationships around me, the promises of God, and the lessons He wants me to learn from the journey. It has made me appreciate the women of strength and love who pour into my spirit, who share their lives with me, who love my children, and fight WITH me for my marriage, my children, my life, and our friendship. They fight FOR me.

These are beautiful women of God who champion growth, maturity, forgiveness and depth of character. They hold me accountable to a higher standard, and their very life sharpens my own. These trials are a maturing process of becoming focused less on ourselves and more on how we can love others well, give generously of what we have, pass over judgment, and give grace.

If you feel invisible, unseen, unknown, or a mark in the crosshairs of a renowned and accomplished marksman, take heart. You're in good company. Courageously remove one foot from the swamp, and then the other. Be mindful of the steep, slippery shoreline lest you fall back into the mud. Graciously extend your hand back to your friend in the muck and mire of a broken relationship. Look in her eyes and genuinely invite her to join you in healthy relationship on the shore. If she cannot stop sifting dirt from water, you must leave her behind.

There is a high price; walking away does not come cheap. But staying is far more costly. The productivity of the seeds of His word is dependent upon the receptiveness of the uncertain soil of the human heart. Cultivating it requires diligence, perseverance, wisdom, and sometimes, a good pruning.

REFLECTION

- What does a true friend mean to you? What are the most important qualities of a true friend?

- Has your intuition ever prompted you to do something and you ignored it or pushed it aside? What happened as a result?

- How can you practice listening to yourself and your intuition? What is one thing or one situation right now where you will commit to trusting yourself?

- What are your tendencies to gravitate to a difficult or toxic relationship? Do you tend to try to fix or sift dirt from water? Do you flee? How does that normal response line up with the voice of your intuition?

- What important lessons (gifts) have you learned from a seasonal or short-term relationship?

9: PRETTY CRAZY
Social Media: My So-Called Life

Understand that the right to choose your own path
is a sacred privilege. Use it.
~Oprah Winfrey

Truth be told, this is a hard chapter for me to write. I wish I could say I was strong enough to resist the psychological battleground that is our social media world; alas, I am not. Quite truthfully, I'm one of its many growing addicts.

Because of the nature of my past with primary female relationships and my experiences with women both growing up and in adulthood, I have struggled in the social world that now operates with every one of us a breath away from bumping into each other every minute of the day. Every friendship, loose-thread relational connection, photo, and word or update is open for interpretation and, far more commonly, misinterpretation.

I've watched people battle on Facebook over political issues, seen them over-share personal or marital concerns, post thinly-veiled aggressive statuses, and verbally harass or attack others' opinions and beliefs. And these people are supposedly friends! I've squinted my eyes and clenched my teeth as I've watched it all play out in the comments of a Facebook status update. Decade-old friendships or new relational connections engage in a veritable food fight over a personal opinion on a news article. It's crazy!

But just like you, I've contributed and been a part of Facebook's demise. Whether by my ignorance, indifference, or silent acquiescence, I, too, have participated when a news feed becomes no better than the pawn of a schoolyard bully. In this brave new world, I have been misunderstood, rejected, criticized, and hurt. And I'm sure I have been an unintentional perpetrator of the same.

FACEBOOK AND FRIENDSHIPS

In the beginning, Facebook was awesome. It started out being harmless and social and really just fun! Catching up with old friends and acquaintances from across a lifetime, family members far away, it was a gathering place to share, connect, and reconnect. It was perfect (minus all the time we lost)!

But quickly Facebook turned grey. It became a place often riddled with both deliberate and unintentional mixed messages, misunderstandings, and passive aggression. It became a gateway drug to insecurity, jealousy, competitiveness, pettiness, bragging, and out-and-out lying . . . and meanness, just plain, old-fashioned meanness. I wonder how we got here. How and why did we give Facebook so much power?

We contemplate and compose status updates about whatever we're doing, and then calculate our worth by the number of likes we get. We send cryptic messages with status updates, wall posts, photos, and what and whom we choose to "like."

In the world of social media, many female friendships have suffered. Some didn't survive.

Several years ago I experienced a painful ending of a friendship that I believe was driven largely by Facebook. What began as a simple misunderstanding quickly grew to staggering levels of distrust and unforgiveness, largely borne of assumptions made by posts, status updates, and coincidental wall messages from friends and acquaintances.

Over the course of a few months, a once dear friendship deteriorated beyond repair. It remains one of the most confusing relational failures of my life, but it is not uncommon. Just in the last month, two of my dear friends have shared their experience with being not only unfriended, but blocked by women they believed were once their friends. Women who, having unresolved feelings toward them and unable or unwilling to express them, chose to block them from even being able to find them on the Facebook network.

The power of social media should not be discounted. Although many of us are unwilling to admit our addictions to them or the hurt and insecurities incurred by them, the numbers tell a much different story.

A FEW RELEVANT STATISTICS

Facebook is the largest online social network. Founded in 2004, the media network reached 1.31 billion active monthly users as of January 1, 2014. On average, 50% of all Facebook users log on in any given day and nearly 80% of Facebook users 18-34 check Facebook first thing in the morning.[14]

These numbers pale in comparison to the staggering statistics I shared with you in chapter 5: that in 2012 there was a 31% increase in cosmetic procedures specifically cited as a result of looking better on social media! To make the assertion that Facebook and other social media are not immensely powerful influencers in today's culture is naïve at best, and otherwise extremely irresponsible and disingenuous.

I propose that Facebook is the number one growing addiction crossing all social and economic boundaries. Unlike many addictions there are few, if any, disincentives to its addictive use. In fact, social relevance is largely dependent on the participation in, and understanding of, social media and we as a culture are becoming more and more afraid to stand against its current.

The power of media has become so great that it threatens to expose our beliefs. If we stand up for someone being harassed, everyone will see. Everyone will know what we believe—what we will and will not stand for. As a result, we become afraid to stand out, afraid to stand apart in a culture hell-bent on the emotional and social destruction of those who disagree with its tenets. It's a dangerous time to stand apart.

COMMON DEFINITIONS AND THEIR UNDERLYING IMPLICATIONS

"Friending" - What is a friend? The advent of social media has really confused our idea of who our friends are. When I was growing up, a friend was a person with whom you had an actual relationship— someone you talked to face to face, with whom you did life, or

shared a common past. In the culture today, we've blurred the line of friendship between an actual friend and an acquaintance.

The reality is we have a very small number of true friends. At the end of the day, you can probably count these people on one hand. Maybe a few more, but it's not likely. The rest, the several hundred or more remaining, are acquaintances! They are people you know, and perhaps truly enjoy. That's great. Really. But they are not true friends.

Clouding the landscape even more, social media presents the opportunity to blur the line further by "friending" people we hardly even know. Some of them we don't really know at all. How many social media "friends" do you have? I know my "friends" number somewhere near 600 and I certainly wouldn't call many of them on the phone to share an intimate story.

They're acquaintances and I care about them, but when and how did the number of friends we have become a competition? Facebook "friending" has become an all-out race to collect the most. I talked to a young woman recently who confessed that she was so addicted to Facebook, she could go into the bathroom at a restaurant and come out with several new "friends!"

It's funny! It really is. But it's also a sad reflection on the state of our lives. For this brave young woman, she confessed it was not only controlling her life, it was slowly tearing apart her marriage. In a moment of realization she determined to take back control. She eliminated the few hundred friends she barely knew from her friend list and got back to engaging in her real life that was right in front of her.

So many of us are not living the real lives that are ours. When we tune out from reality and tune in to social media or reality television, we're missing out on the REAL that is happening right in front of us, masquerading around in our so-called lives.

"Liking" - What do we "like" on Facebook? If you're paying attention you will notice people are becoming more and more discriminating about what and whom they "like." We know people are watching us; everything we do is so public. While we're careful and becoming more and more savvy about how we operate, by now, we know how things work and we've learned how to play some pretty mean games.

We send subliminal messages to people when we choose to "like" or ignore their status update. We might pretend we didn't see it or say we weren't online, but when we "like" a status, we send a message. When it's our birthday and people send us messages and we "like" all of them but one, it sends a message. Like non-verbal communication, sometimes our absence speaks louder than our participation. Facebook has become the ultimate playground for passive-aggressive behavior.

If all of this seems crazy, and makes me sound crazy, then I'm doing a good job! I've felt crazy and I've talked to dozens of women who have felt crazy too. It *is* crazy! And yet it's painfully true.

"De-facing" - Here's a new social media term for the dictionaries: de-facing. I define it as: *the art of passive-aggressively inflicting emotional harm on another person by intentionally hurtful or indifferent behavior, all the while pretending it is inadvertent or unknown.*

Been there? Intentionally or not, we have all been guilty of de-facing one of our many "friends" on Facebook or other social media. I would venture a guess that most often, it's someone we know well. Perhaps we are having a personal struggle with someone—we're jealous or harboring resentment or ill will toward them.

Unsure of how to remedy the relational problem, we begin to ignore them or post subtle status updates that we know will get under their skin: Photos with other friends in an attempt to incite jealousy or messages that only that person will see and question our motive. We may play coy, but it's pretty transparent. We're attempting to de-face our friend and there's nothing pretty about it.

But, the inevitable outcome of this behavior is that eventually it backfires on us. While we attempt to deface our friend or make them feel small (consciously or not), we actually begin to destroy our own integrity because, despite our denials, deep down we know what we're doing.

Sure, most likely we will succeed in hurting our friend. That was, after all, our original intent. What we didn't intend was the backlash to ourselves. Regardless, the ultimate result is that this unhealthy and hurtful behavior will catch up to us. Time is not a frequent liar.

After awhile, our friend and others will catch on. We can only present false sincerity for so long before our real motives start slipping through the cracks in the façade. Our attempts to destroy someone's worth by passive-aggressive behavior on social media will at some point intersect with our real lives.

We can hide behind our devices for a time, but eventually we have to face the person we pretend we're not hurting. Sooner or later we have to account for our actions and realize we've lost not only a petty game, but also a friend.

"Unfriending" - What a loaded term. In today's culture, unfriending has become one of the most powerfully known ways to deliver the ultimate dis. I've had and I've heard real conversations about unfriending and, within the groups I travel, it's a weighty decision. There are definite implications to the seemingly simple, single-click decision to unfriend someone.

So is it ever okay to unfriend a person on Facebook?

The short answer is yes. Of course it is. This is not to say I am encouraging or advocating a massive unfriending on your Facebook today . . . unless they are people you hardly even know! The simple truth is every one of us can call a name or a face to mind that has hurt you, or is continuing to hurt you on social media. Only you know what you hear in the deepest place in your heart about your situation; I'm just saying it's okay if you choose to eliminate the access that person has to you online.

One of the biggest problems with social media and networks like Facebook is we become so accustomed to our own little insulated world. We forget that each "friend" has a face. Each, a story, a past, and a broken life just like ours. As tough as we try to be on the outside, we're all pretty tender on the inside. When the lights are off and the computer is shut down, we're the same, you and me.

Some of us are tired of the games and don't want to play anymore. As we get stronger and braver and truer to our real self, we find the strength to put our foot down when it comes to petty schoolyard games, even though they're now happening on a bigger playground. We begin seeing past the veneer and start practicing courage. We were made for more than this crazy so-called life. We were made to be real.

We are designed by a Creator to be real people with real friends and real emotions, having real experiences and a desire to grow and learn and be free! Life is hard enough on its own, we need friends who encourage us to be better, and love us for who we are, friends who accept us wherever we are in our journey. Those who tear at our hearts, gossip behind our backs, or criticize our dreams are not our friends.

We need to be discerning. We've got to be able to

distinguish the real friend from the false one, the true friend from the acquaintance, and the encourager from the critic.

With the crazy games that go on every day, sometimes unfriending isn't an insult at all. Sometimes, it's the greatest gift you can give to yourself. Surprisingly, it can be a gift to the offender too.

We teach people how to treat us, and for most women, we let the bar fall far too low. I've certainly been there. I've been in relationships where I've let the threshold for acceptable behavior hover right around ground level. Who am I kidding? There are times I've let the bar just lay there on the floor. It hurts.

Often, repeat offenders don't realize their behavior is so poor or hurtful. Perhaps they've gotten away with it time after time and no one has held them accountable. No one has found the courage to stand their ground, and unfortunately the offender has never reached the bottom. When you put your foot down on the behavior you will not tolerate, you raise the bar. Maybe your silent decision will present a learning opportunity for them, maybe not. But it will surely present one for you. Removing toxic or negative people from your circle of influence is the first step to designing an unhindered life. We need encouragers if we're going to live this life well.

You were made with a purpose that only you can fulfill in the unique and beautiful way God made you. You need friendships that will spur you on to find your best self. You should have friends who encourage you to reach beyond your grasp so you find out what it truly means to grow.

So often we want others to stand up for us, to fight for us, but what we really desire in the deepest recesses of our hearts is to have the courage to stand up for ourselves. Fight for you! Fight for your dream, your life, this life! You only get one. Prove to yourself you have what it takes. Fight for you.

HOW TO MAKE SOCIAL MEDIA
ADD VALUE TO YOUR LIFE

With all this talk about social media and it's crazy passive-aggressive games, who would want it? The truth is, these networks can be far more positive than negative. The power lies with each of us and how we design it—how we navigate the common and predictable pitfalls and make it add value to our lives. Social media can be a powerful tool to add value, but you've got to be smart and you've got to be brave.

First, look at your friends and your feeds. The people who are hurting or annoying you have to go. If you don't want to unfriend them, just unfollow them on your feed where they can't provoke you. Follow people, pages, and blogs that are positive and inspirational, that make you think and feel better about your life.

I believe you get to design your life. You certainly get to design your newsfeed! Choose with intention. Choose wisely! It doesn't mean you don't love and care for the people you stop showing in your newsfeed. If they constantly get you down or make you feel bad about your life or yourself, that's not healthy! You must intentionally choose the people you allow to influence your life.

Second, be an example. Be thoughtful. Be courteous. Remember to ask yourself: *Is it truthful? Is it helpful? Is it inspiring, fun, or necessary? Is it kind?* If not, then don't post it!

Accept the reality that it's pretty certain we will at some point unintentionally hurt someone because of a photo or status post. We can't know what every person is going through and what we might say that accidentally offends, irritates, or picks at a wound. What we're talking about here is intentionality and patterns of behavior.

You know your heart and your motives. You know if you're posting something to hurt another person or if you're just excited about something happening in your world. You have a right to be happy about your life and share it! Be free.

Third, be you. Be unapologetically and unmistakably you. This most certainly is the hardest part and requires a bit more grit. I honestly can't say I've got it down myself or ever truly will, but I know the process begins by living with our whole hearts. It's the scary thing but it's always the right thing.

When we come from a place of wholeness, no matter what we say in our status update or in our conversations with others, we know we are enough. No matter the number of "likes" or the response from the other person, we are confident in ourselves. We know our truth, we accept our failures, missteps, and mistakes and feel safe in our own skin.

Wholeness comes from living authentically and real even when it's hard—especially when it's hard. When we lean into the discomfort, we find our true selves, the truest part of our selves. It's when we reveal our flawed, humble, and vulnerable selves and say "Here I am, this is me." And if someone doesn't "like" it, that's okay. If someone won't forgive us, we can still be whole.

We are more than our likes, more than our number of friends, more . . . so much more than this crazy social media world we live in. We've got to fight to be real in an unreal reality and boldly design an unhindered life. You've got this.

REFLECTION

- Is social media taking up more time or room in your life than you would like to admit?

- Have you experienced or witnessed the dissolution of a relationship on social media or one directly or indirectly because of social media?

- Is there a person or group of people who continually hurt you on social media? What stops you from unfollowing or unfriending this person?

- How can you begin to design your news feed to add value to your life? What is one thing you will commit to doing right now to that end?

10: PRETTY UNFORGIVING
A Root of Bitterness

We can only learn to love by loving.
~Iris Murdoch

Do you have someone in your life that you just can't forgive? You know the one who comes to mind—the one who caused deep, searing wounds in the tender places of your soul. These are the wounds that reach down into the very core of your spirit, splitting you in two. You think you've forgiven them; you think you've moved on, but the trigger is so easily tripped and you face plant. You fall flat to the ground like it's happening again. I know this is happening when something seemingly insignificant or trivial quickly has me spiraling into self-doubt, anger, and shame. Suddenly an old wound becomes very fresh.

We pretend we're fine; on the surface everything looks great. But the pain is there, trapped just beneath the surface of a put-together life. Outwardly religious, inwardly rebellious. Somewhere buried in our subconscious, we think the rules don't apply to us. The pain we know doesn't fit the requirements of forgiveness. Not us. Not that person. Not our situation. Not this time.

But the wounds we carry hold a power far beyond the hurt in our hearts. It holds the power to grow a thick, gnarly root of bitterness in the fertile soil of our hearts. We tend and nurture that bitter root every time we withhold forgiveness, carry a grudge, gossip, stereotype, exclude others, and seek our own way. It grows even deeper when we seek our happiness and pleasure at the expense of another.

The root is so powerful that we can lash out at others who have nothing to do with our pain—people who simply remind us of something we fear, something we know, something we despise in ourselves. We all know these people. We've all been in relationship with these people. We have all been these people.

Every circumstance and trial in our lives gives us the opportunity to choose. Will we grow and become better through the trials of life, or will we allow them to make us bitter, resentful, angry, unforgiving, cold? Will we press into relationship or withdraw and isolate? Will we plant seeds of life, or seeds of a bitter, critical spirit?

It's human nature to bristle when we come face to face with an old wound, when we turn around and find the person who hurt us standing before us. What I struggle with most is how to live out the Bible.

Scripture doesn't give us a How-To guide when it comes to the specific, day-in and day-out of relationship. It doesn't give us a script to use when we run into the one who has caused us pain. It doesn't give us a play-by-play on what to do when we trip over ourselves and our selfishness. Although it offers direction and guidance, it is widely interpreted and in some situations it seems there is freedom to go either way. Do we err on the side of grace or speak a hard truth? When does love and tolerance cross the line into wisdom and discernment? When we honestly just don't know how to take a single step forward in a relationship that has come to a dead end, we want a clear sign telling us which way to go and there isn't one. We don't have a flow chart. But we do have this: love.

Love one another; for love covers a multitude of sins. And I know that sounds trite and naïve because I, too, have had relationships that have stalled, flat lined, and there seems to be no earthly way of moving forward. But I know that we must choose against bitterness. We must literally fight against bitterness.

If we claim to have any faith at all, we must choose love. And choosing love doesn't mean relationship. Love doesn't mean we walk back in. It doesn't mean we forget. It doesn't mean it didn't happen and we aren't thankful that the journey brought us out. It just means we continue to love, even if that has to be from a distance.

We choose the best for them and for us, for this time. We refuse to give in to the persistent invitations to bitterness, the whispered lies tempting us to join in the folly. It's a fool's game and one I've joined in too many times.

Instead, we wait. We listen to our hearts. We become aware of our pain; we seek and find healing so we don't lash out at someone else and become the bitter, critical spirit. We consciously choose love so that in our honest pursuit of freedom and holiness, we don't subconsciously leave a wake of destruction in our paths. We must choose, over and over again because, by nature, we're prone to acts of emotional violence. The words we speak carry a heavy weight and have the power to destroy a spirit, a hope, a life.

CHOOSING LOVE

So how do we choose love? How do we respond in kindness when our heart just doesn't feel it? When all we really want to do is seek vengeance, we must consciously and deliberately choose to go against our feelings. Choose to respond, instead of react. Choose to be kind instead of repaying in kind.

Too often we're driven by our feelings—our desire to retaliate or defend ourselves. I know my instant reaction is rarely, if ever, grace. Far more often it's anger and vengeance. It's never wise to react quickly when we've been injured or are facing a wound from our past. Take time so you can respond, instead of react.

WAITING ON GOD

Have you ever found yourself in a season of wait? Have you faced a situation or time where you could not plow forward or fix it on your own and had to wait on God to coordinate, orchestrate, and somehow make a way? For much of my life I've been a runner. Whether on the pavement, in relationships, or personal challenges, if I saw something I wanted I dove in head first and made my way as quickly and efficiently as possible. That doesn't mean it always turned out right. Far too often I went off making my own way, and I've learned that the faster I run in the wrong direction the farther I have to make my way back. But despite all the ways in which I have fought and sought to prove myself capable, to prove myself genuine, my greatest lessons have been the quiet moments inside the cavernous walls of "impossible" where God whispered to the still places of my heart: *Wait.*

I look back over a life and see an endless track record of His faithfulness: Unanswered prayers, unforgiveness, heartaches, and heartbreak. At these times I wondered and pleaded and begged: *Where are you God? Do you even see me? Do you care?* But every time I've faithfully waited on God, and even when I haven't, He has come through for me.

Each of the impossible goals, difficult relationships, and seasons of hardship happened in the order and timing of a God who knows what lies ahead and prepares the way. Each challenge or experience builds on the strength gained from the one before. Each lesson charts the way for the challenge ahead. And one of the most beautiful things I have learned about wait is its marriage to hope. In order to wait we must believe there is something to wait *for*, and hope is a revolutionary patience.

I'm beginning to believe that wait is one of the greatest lessons we can ever learn. To sit in the silence of the unwritten story and find comfort in that space, this is the intimate juncture where we find our faith. Softening hearts, preparing minds, opening dialogues, whispering truths, choosing love—He is the One who makes the impossible possible. He is the One who makes the way.

Sometimes we just need to be still. And wait.

WITH OUR WORDS AND ACTIONS

Be careful with your words. Be cautious in your actions. So many eyes are watching our moves, listening to our voices, and surveying the rhythm of our lives. Each of us is a teacher—to our children, nieces, granddaughters, neighbors, and friends. We teach the next generation of women how to treat other women.

It seems that critics with their judgment, ridicule, rejection, and just plain meanness rise to the surface of everyday life. These people are so easy to find. And though we know in our hearts that all these things overflow from a bitter and jealous heart, it hurts just the same. God made us to live in community, to have soft hearts toward one another. And if we live true to the nature He created, it hurts deeply.

We were made to be free, and yet we live enslaved to idols of acceptance, inclusion, affirmation, and someone else's love. We coach ourselves to be strong, to thicken our skin, to put up walls, to walk away, and to hate them back. This world teaches us to be more like them to save ourselves. But I'd rather be broken.

I'd rather be broken and tattered and torn in two, than to close off the part of me that makes me soft: the most powerful, beautiful part of ourselves—our princess heart—the Fruit of the Spirit. This is the very beating breath that makes us different from those who mock, those who judge and live with a bitter, critical spirit. It's the tattered and threadbare who are real. The ones with enough courage to let the things of this life break them, and let Him rebuild them whole.

> Therefore, as God's chosen people, holy and dearly loved, clothe yourselves with compassion, kindness, humility, gentleness, and patience. Bear with each

other and forgive whatever grievances you may have against one another. Forgive as the Lord forgave you. And over all these virtues, put on love, which binds them all together in perfect unity.

—Colossians 3:12-14

The challenge, and the higher calling, is to choose love. One of the greatest battles we wage in this life is the fight against bitterness. And love is the bravest, fiercest fighter of all.

I want to leave a legacy of love, a legacy of kindness, gentleness, and peace. I do not want a love that lies down, because I don't believe that is love. Love is strong. Love is powerful. It sets healthy boundaries and grows exponentially the more you practice. Let us be people of love, a community of loving well. Offering grace when none is deserved because undeserved grace is the truest and rarest grace of all.

When you don't know how to move forward, choose love. When there seems to be no earthly way of moving on, choose love.

REFLECTION

- Put a name and a face to the person in your life you have a hard time forgiving.

- How has living with unforgiveness kept you from moving forward into a full and wholehearted life?

- In your life, do you typically wait on God or do you struggle with wait and force your own way? How has that played out? What have you learned?

- How can you be more intentional in choosing love with your words and actions in a difficult relationship right now?

PART FOUR
LOOKING FORWARD

11: PRETTY FREE
The Only Way

Life is a petty thing
unless it is moved by the indomitable urge to extend its boundaries.
~Jose Ortega Y Gassett

If we know we must choose love and it's a bona fide war against our flesh, how do we do it? How do we live well in a world full of pain, hurt, and highly erected walls of protection with no instructions? Everyone wants a How-To guide, but the reality is it doesn't work. Think of all the ways we know how-to and yet we don't-do. We know how to lose weight but we don't want to do it. We know many ways to stop our addictions and yet we don't even try. How-to doesn't help us if we don't really want to. And even if we wanted to with everything that we have, there's no how-to when it comes to relationships, love, and forgiveness. That is how we come to grace.

GRACE UNCOMMON

The reality of our existence is that we are saved by grace. Not by acts, so that none can boast, but by grace. (see Ephesians 2:8-9)

So what is grace? Grace is honor or favor granted by someone who need not do so. Simply put, grace is undeserved mercy. It's a lot to process, really—far too much for the selfish, judgmental human mind to comprehend.

The idea of grace, the desire of grace, the very will of grace will always lead me to the heart of forgiveness. And forgiveness is a tricky thing. It's problematic and complex because we, by nature, are so demanding, self-centered, and proud. Maybe I shouldn't speak for you, but I can certainly speak for myself and I've been in many situations that required forgiveness—asking for it, as well as giving it when it wasn't asked for. There are times where it seemed that an apology wasn't even considered, when forgiveness wasn't about the other person at all, but to set myself free. And the truth is we're either ready or we're not.

There are three options in any conflict requiring forgiveness: in, out, or wait. And where we are tells us a lot about the condition of our hearts.

OPTION ONE: WAIT

You wait. For something or someone—some word or action, an apology or occurrence. You wait for time to pass. Something. Anything. Maybe nothing. You wait, for whatever it is you feel you cannot proceed without. And then when it happens, if it happens, you come back to this place to determine again whether "it" was good enough. We're all the same.

OPTION TWO: OUT

When you take the "Out" option, you walk away. You sever communication, cut ties, pack up your bags, and go home. You pretend. You try to convince yourself and others that the ache in your heart isn't really hurting and you fake it. You move on, but really your heart is still sitting back in the very place you left it. You stop growing.

Chances are you suffer deeply from the invisible wounds of bitterness and unforgiveness that war against all that you know in your heart to be true and all you were created to be. But you're just not ready to accept, acknowledge, or deal with the pain. Not yet.

OPTION THREE: IN

When you choose the "In" option, you dive in and do the work. You choose love. You choose to respond and not react. You choose to stop trying to control the situation, the other person, and the outcome. You realize how far and how often you fall short, and you choose to extend grace. You choose to be uncommon.

Common people hold the status quo. They fight and they intimidate, they gossip, demean, and destroy. They harbor unforgiveness and love to cast blame. You are not common. Together, we're the uncommon: the ones who choose the less traveled road of living with our whole hearts. Living in the reality of our messy lives, we choose grace every day. We choose love.

> Finally, brothers and sisters, whatever is true, whatever is noble, whatever is right, whatever is pure, whatever is lovely, whatever is admirable – if anything is excellent or praiseworthy – think about such things. —Phil. 4:8

Rarely will we find a person who pleases us all the time. Even then, their time is limited. We fall in love or meet our best friend and they can do no wrong . . . perhaps for a week. And then our messy humanness comes oozing out from the cracks and we're busted. We bump into one another. We hurt others and we get hurt back.

If we're "In" we're willing to work it out and make it right. We're willing to sacrifice some of our fragile feelings to speak truth in love. We make the effort, knowing the other person's feelings are just as valid as our own. We choose to believe that our imperfect progress is still progress and we fight for something we cannot see, and yet still believe is true.

In, out, or wait. Where do you find yourself? I ask because I know you're in the midst of something and you find yourself in one of these places. Or you're uninvolved but trying to help from the periphery, which means you're still involved. You're kind of in. Watching. Waiting. You have one foot precariously close to the line and you're praying for both parties to be in. But one is in and one is out . . . it's delicate, and yet so fierce.

Moving on, getting out, waiting, supposedly indifferent, yet bitter to the core. More often than not, we just throw rocks at each other until nothing remains but a banged up, dented in vestige of a relationship. Something that was once of great value has been destroyed by our very own hands, crushed by our own stubborn, bitter, critical spirits.

We need to be willing to forgive ourselves and others who have hurt us so we can move forward into health. We must move from being common and ordinary, to being women willing to lead a movement of change—women willing to be uncommon, extending grace, offering forgiveness, and seeking peace despite circumstances. We must be women who encourage, support, inspire, and love other women.

Forgiveness is vital to even thinking about the next chapter of this book. Truly, it's the only way. Unfortunately, there really is no way to move into an unhindered life if you're stuck in the bitter unrest that is unforgiveness.

Have the courage to go in. *All in!* Roll up your sleeves and do the work. It's good work—painful, healing, necessary work.

God can mend and redeem our brokenness, but He's far more interested in the transformation of our hearts. He cares more about our character than our comfort. He desires for us to have soft hearts, to be teachable, and He wants to show us that through our trials He can carve in us the very heart of God.

STUMBLING ON GRACE

Things go around and come around and never, ever run in a straight line. We hurt one another because of our own embroiled bitterness, insecurity, and pain. When bad things happen we blame karma, and we often pray people get what they deserve. So many of us pretend we're okay when we're really just experts at hiding how we feel.

And though this life is never simple, and certainly never pain free, despite karma or consequence it always works out in the end. Complex and complicated, damaged and torn we stand. Together, apart, arms outstretched, wrapped around or holding at length. We battle. We love and we hate and everything in between.

But time passes and life evolves. Battles are fought and hard lessons learned. Relationships and people change. And somewhere down the road of life we eventually stumble upon grace. We stumble because I do not believe we can find it on our own. Grace is, after all, undeserved mercy.

It is those people, those times, those circumstances that give rise to our innate desire for vengeance and retaliation. To give grace is so contrary to our nature that it cannot be of ourselves. Any possibility of giving undeserved mercy surely requires the divine assistance of a supernatural God.

Grace allows us to forgive someone who never asked for forgiveness, who never even said they were sorry. It allows us to choose to act with a spirit of love and kindness in the face of continued hostility. It allows us to truly encourage and lift up another soul with a pure heart.

We find grace, not because we're noble or righteous, but because we realize how much we need it ourselves. We've learned by trial and error that holding the burden of anger and unforgiveness only wearies our already tired heart.

And because I've seen redemption so clearly in hardened hearts, nearly broken marriages, and bitter feuds: I'm convinced that as surely as the sun rises in the morning and sets in the evening, He will have His way with us.

In whatever way He must break us to give in to grace, He will. In whatever way He must strip us, so He can mold us to Him, He will. It is not a question of when, but how. And at what cost?

How long will we hold onto stubborn pride before we just let Him do His work in us?

When we find grace, a weight is lifted that frees us to love others well despite how they treat us. We begin to look past the person who hurt us and see their own pain, feel their own crushing loss. It's when you look back and see the redemption story—how you never, ever should have been the one, and yet there you are, giving grace, sharing sorrow, encouraging hope, and choosing love—that you understand grace. You see the person and realize all along they were just looking for grace. It's all grace. Every bit of this life.

Walk away if you must, but love. Bitterness only burdens your already weary heart and you were called to be free. He will have His way with us; that is a promise. And somewhere, someday, you will look back and see redemption's story and be grateful.

Step up, stand up, show up. Go *all in* and choose grace. Fight for the freedom that only comes through the mercy of forgiveness. Everything you desire hinges on it.

REFLECTION

- How have you been the recipient of grace (undeserved mercy) in your life?

- How did it change or impact the trajectory of your life or your story?

- Is there someone who holds power over you because you cannot find it in your heart to forgive?

- What might happen if you decided to go *all in?*

12: PRETTY BOLD
Boldly Designing Unhindered Lives

Character cannot be developed in ease and quiet.
Only through experience of trial and suffering
can the soul be strengthened, vision cleared, ambition inspired,
and success achieved.
~Helen Keller

A s I sit down to write this chapter I am faced with the inner conviction that I do not know the way. In looking back, looking in, and looking out I share the story of my life. Every chapter holds an intimate part of who I am, ways I have struggled, and how I have determined to overcome. These are the ways I have chosen to put my faith in a power that is far greater than I.

These are the crossroads of a life—the critical junctures where we decide to trust in ourselves or put our faith in something greater than us. We choose to believe there is a plan beyond what we can see and a purpose fashioned out of our greatest weakness to make us stronger.

I guess you could say that my story has been a journey of boldly designing an unhindered life. From the time I was a young girl I've struggled with more than my fair share of hindrances, often finding myself tripping over my own two feet.

And so who am I to tell you how to design an unhindered life? The truth is, I am no one. I am not an expert and I'm certainly not perfect. I don't even get it right in my own life as often as I'd like. The truth is I cannot be your guide.

But I believe that we are more alike than we are different, and so I'd like to be your companion. I believe you struggle with similar insecurities and worries; I believe you set yourself up for similarly unrealistic expectations of perfection, and mistreat yourself when you inevitably fall short. And so this chapter begins a life-long journey of faith.

THROW OFF WHAT HINDERS

By nature, experience, and social conditioning women often tend toward exclusive, competitive, and superficial behaviors with other women. Instead of living open, wholehearted, and authentic, we hide behind walls, under layers of masks and confusing games. Of course we're triggered. Of course we stumble. Of course we fall short of the expectations of perfection that we hold for ourselves in a world so broken and bitter and mean.

Therefore, since we are surrounded by such a great cloud of witnesses, let us throw off everything that hinders and the sin that so easily entangles, and let us run with perseverance the race marked out for us.

—Hebrews 12:1

Start where you are. The path that lies before us is long. The course is unpredictable and the way unknown. For many of us we're holding heartaches as old as ourselves and wounds that over the course of a lifetime have left an indelible mark. I know what you're thinking: *You couldn't possibly understand. Not this. Not my pain. Not what has happened to me.* You're right, I can't. But He does. And He is your guide.

You cannot begin a journey without taking the first step. God will meet you in your suffering, but you have to move. The Red Sea didn't part until Moses stepped out in faith. He believed that God would deliver them. "Do not be afraid. Stand firm and you will see the deliverance the Lord will bring you today. The Lord will fight for you; you need only to be still." (Exodus 14:13-14)

As women we're so prone to fear and comparison that before we even get started we're looking down the road to see who's ahead of us. Too often we abandon the journey right there at the start because we're afraid to compete. If we can't do it better, then we'd rather not try.

We're also afraid to fail. Though our lives aren't perfect, they're ours. Broken and damaged and riddled with scars, we fear accepting what *is* might be better than risking what could *be*.

We've lost our confidence over years of critical or damaging relationships, hurtful comments, and rejections from those we loved. We've lost respect for ourselves over decisions we've made and the lives we have lived. We fear starting something new because we don't even know how to begin. Perhaps we're surrounded by others who continue to pull us down and hinder our imperfect progress. We're afraid we just don't know how to fight.

But this isn't our battle to fight or our road to pave. When we live by faith and with a vision further than ourselves, when we live by a standard of grace, we realize He fights with us. For us. He told us to be still. We discover that the path that lies before us was planned from the beginning, and He has already gone before us and made a way.

When we live by faith, we believe in advance that He will give us His strength to overcome our weakness. We believe He will meet us in our moments of failure and speak truth, in the midst of the clamoring noise, to the center of our soul.

We know we cannot do it by our own strength, and we will never do it perfectly. But when we become real, when we accept our hardship and our pain as the greatest part of us, we realize that an extraordinary life is charted imperfectly by faith.

THE OBEDIENCE OF FAITH

Faith is not defined by an inner attitude. Faith requires action and it proves itself genuine by obedience. Through trial, testing, and the stripping and sifting of those things we cling to for security and safety in this world we make our way to faith. When we're brought face to face with our deepest insecurities, fear, and anxiety, when we resist the raging desire to flee we encounter faith. When we press in to relationship, pain, and hurt instead of pulling back in isolation and fear, and when we continue pushing forward, one bold step after another, toward the realization of our dreams we stumble upon faith.

A broken past is healed only by holding unswervingly to the hope of an assured future. Believing that He who promised us is faithful. This is a journey of strength and steadfastness, charted through the treacherous territory of setting firm boundaries, gracefully walking away from toxic or unhealthy relationships, and pressing in to loving, safe people who encourage and spur us to love freely and with our whole hearts. These are the people who redefine acceptance, grace, forgiveness, and love in a world overflowing with bitterness and pain—friends who build us up and push us to find the best that is in us. They encourage us to find the strength that lies hidden, just beneath our fear.

Living boldly demands that we design our lives with intention or we risk missing the point. There is no way around it: in this life we will have trial. We will face pain, we will be rejected, and we will be tempted to lose heart. But we will always have a choice.

We can be bold and brave; we can face our adversaries and speak truth and love. We can allow the hurt to make us stronger, the lies weaker, the circle smaller, and the friendships deeper. We can unshackle ourselves from the things that try to hold us back and have always fought to hold us back. We can design our lives to be free from bondage, to be bold and unhindered if we believe that we can. He made us for more than a superficial life. It's up to us to believe it and fight for it.

With hearts made for eternity, sometimes it's hard to live in this broken world. In times of trial, confusion, silence, and pain do not throw away your confidence. Do not fall prey to the lie that isolation and protectionism will save you. Persevere. Press in. Lean on safe, loving relationships. Walk shoulder to shoulder and carry each other's burdens. Two are better than one.

Seek relationships where grace, truth, and forgiveness are the standard. Cultivate and practice your faith. Do not rely on emotion and feeling because the heart is deceitful above all things. Those who believe in Him and trust in His faithfulness will be rewarded.

We were not made to simply withstand the trials of this life—to exist in them until the darkness lifts or to shrink back and be discouraged and destroyed. No. We were made to persevere, to stand our ground in the face of suffering, and to triumph over darkness. Against all odds.

REFLECTION

- What are the crossroads of your life?

- Where do you find the juncture between trusting in your self and having a faith that is bigger than you?

- In this chapter I stated, "You cannot begin a journey without taking the first step . . . [and that] Faith proves itself by obedience." What is your first step of obedience?

13: PRETTY STRONG
Wait for Great

Bid me run,
and I will strive with things impossible.
~William Shakespeare

When I was only twenty years old I married my high school sweetheart. I had just turned twenty-two when we divorced. When my rebound relationship ended a year later, I had to grieve the loss of both relationships at once because I had never allowed myself time to recover from the first. A virtual flood of emotions rushed at me like a crushing wave. The pain and overwhelming feelings I had stuffed and pretended didn't hurt me for all of my life brought me to my knees.

That's the thing about grief. It waits.

For so many years I felt rejected and abandoned. I just didn't understand. *Why? Why had all these relational failures happened to me? Why were so many of my experiences so painful?*

For the next two years I began a radical journey to the heart of my soul. Finally facing my grief, I decided that I would learn to love myself regardless of who loved me back. I made the commitment that I would learn to be strong, whatever that meant and at whatever cost. I would finish my college degree so I could take care of myself if my dream of becoming a wife never came true for me and if my greatest desire of being a mom never actually happened.

At the end of two life-changing, mind-bending years, I tested myself by backpacking through Europe for seven weeks. Alone. I went to law school and met my amazing husband in a chance encounter at Starbucks. I studied International Human Rights Law for a summer in Ireland.

It's been over twelve years since I set out on that adventure and a lot has happened. Many things I hoped for never did. But I learned that what God had in store for me was far greater than anything I could ever have imagined on my own. I learned that I could still find joy in the middle of heartache and peace in the midst of a storm. I learned that the only way to find healing is by walking step after difficult step through the center of crushing pain.

At the beginning of this book I told you the story would never change. No matter how healthy or secure we are, or how firmly we place our identity in Christ, we will be tested by this life. We will have critics—people who lie to us and about us, people who will never be satisfied with who we are, and that's okay. Regardless of our failures, shortcomings, or imperfections I have learned that in life we have to do the hard work. We have to face the fears we don't want to face and stand before the memories that try to haunt us. We must look in the face of our deepest insecurities and say, "Not this time. Not today. You don't know me anymore <u>because I have changed</u>. And I am not afraid."

It was never easy and it still rarely is—this waiting on God while it all works out. But I learned the awesome power of surrender when I realized that I could only do my part. I finally accepted that for the rest I would have to wait. Wait for great.

SERENITY PRAYER

One of the most powerful tools I leaned on during those extremely life-changing years was the "Serenity Prayer." I've never been able to understand why nearly all the versions of the "Serenity Prayer" leave the most powerful part out. I think it's safe to say nearly everyone has heard the most familiar part of the "Serenity Prayer" at some time in life, but few I know have ever heard the entire thing. It became my rock and my strength.

For two years it sat on my dresser in a frame reminding me how to live each day, each moment. Sometimes all I had strength for was just one breath. I couldn't imagine a day or a week or a month or a year. All I had was this, and the entire Serenity Prayer, to comfort me and remind me that this, this moment, this was enough.

> God grant me the serenity to accept the things I cannot change; courage to change the things I can; and the wisdom to know the difference. Living one day at a time; enjoying one moment at a time; accepting hardship as the pathway to peace; taking, as He did, this sinful world as it is, not as I would have it; trusting that He will make all things right if I surrender to His will; that I may be reasonably happy in this life and supremely happy with Him forever in the next.[15]
>
> —Reinhold Niebuhr

We face difficult seasons and we all go through pain. But the testing of our faith develops perseverance, and learning to accept our broken lives carves out character. Surrendering our life to the One who knows the deepest desires of our heart—and longs to give them to us—paves the imperfect path to peace.

The dreams I wanted to come true were never really the dreams of my heart. The relationships I wished had been different crafted the person that I am today. This life, this earthly, broken, sinful life is not our home. Our hearts were made for eternity; it's why we will never be satisfied living in this world.

With our eyes fixed on the horizon, we see that eternity waits for us, beckons us, commands us to live this life well and with intention. Step by painful step we walk toward a Father with outstretched hands, calling us home. Molding us to Him, He creates in us a deep, enduring, abiding need for His love, His grace, His mercy, and His faithfulness. Now, far more often my question is not *why*, but *for what?*

I've learned that there is always a reason hidden somewhere deep inside the pain—a lesson to learn, a reason to grow, a stronghold to break or an idol to shake. Even if what we've been through should never have happened, we get to decide if we let it haunt us or help us.

We never leave our past behind; we can't. A part of it is always with us, threatening to hold us back. But when we make peace with it, accept it for what it was and not what we wanted it to be, then we get to rewrite our story. We get to design how far it will propel us forward to the life we were created to live.

BUILDING YOU STRONG

We have the power to use some of the greatest challenges in this life to build ourselves strong, but we've got to be willing to work.

I believe we are spiritual beings, but for me, finding my strength in any area of life will always be connected to my physical body—work, sweat, determination—pushing myself harder and further than I thought possible.

There is an integral connection, feeling my heartbeat pounding in my chest, moving from a shallow faith near the shore, which requires no risks and offers no rewards, to a deeper commitment to God. When my feet no longer touch and I feel I'm in way over my head, that's when I know I'm in the right place.

I believe that no matter what trials I face in this life, no matter what hardships, difficulties, heartaches, and pain I encounter, He will make the impossible possible. I believe that with hard work, discipline, and determination, He will build me strong so my life will reflect the goodness of His grace.

HUMBLE BEGINNINGS

Growing up I was no athlete. In fact, I nearly flunked out of gym class my eighth grade year. Back in those days the most strenuous thing we did was a mean game of dodgeball. Which, now that I think of it, really was a mean game!

For the first twenty years of my life I had no real interest in anything athletic. I went out for the track team and even tried cross-country, but it wasn't because I wanted to run. Between plaguing feelings of inferiority and my intense fear of failure, I believed it was better to watch from the sidelines. It wasn't that

I didn't want to compete; deep in my subconscious I was afraid I'd fall short. I was afraid I wouldn't be good and it would only add to my insecurities.

But life happened. I graduated from high school, married my high school sweetheart, and started a life far from the schoolyard. But things didn't get easier. Problems just got more complicated. On the heels of an unanticipated divorce, I found myself moving back in with my parents. Soon after, my broken heart followed me into a new relationship. And when that one suddenly and painfully ended, I came face to face with my reality: I had always placed my hope, my future, my security, and my dreams in the hands of another.

I so desperately wanted to be loved that I was willing to do anything and be anyone. I didn't even know who I was anymore. Maybe I never did. So, I started to run.

In the midst of brokenness and overwhelming hopelessness, running began to center my spirit and calm my anxious heart. It allowed me to begin learning to put the "Serenity Prayer" into action in my life by taking one day at a time, one moment at a time, one intentional step at a time.

Knowing there were days I didn't even want to get out of bed, I slept in my running clothes. I set my alarm just before the sun came up and hit the street before I fully woke up and could convince myself not to go. Running was the way I set my day with intention. Running was how I survived and processed the emotional pain.

I didn't set out with a goal. I didn't wear a watch or a timer. I didn't record my miles or measure my distance. I ran for the sake of running—for the freedom I felt in the moment, for the breath that filled my lungs.

Life never goes forward in a straight, even line. It's messy and unruly and jagged and torn. And there is beauty in the broken and much love in the mess. Despite it all, and because of it all, it is ours.

Feet on pavement, rhythm and timing. Dark and light, stillness and sound. Meditation in the silence carried on the breath of wind. To run: to go steadily without restraint. For me, running is therapy. It is the time I move forward. I set my path and everything fades. In the moment it's just me—the day that is given and my open hand to receive it.

WORK

People say it should be easy. You know those people: the ones who start something only to give up at the first sign of difficulty. They convince themselves and try to convince you that it should be easy and that if we're truly talented or gifted it should come naturally, without effort. But it isn't true. It has never been true.

You look around at the greatest icons, athletes, and innovators in history and they worked hard. I'm not talking about the movie stars or reality television imposters of this time. I'm talking about the real leaders—the brave teachers of a time long past whose words and life live on—those who carved out room in the soul of man because they fought and they bled and they failed and they tried.

Not satisfied with an ordinary life, they worked to make it extraordinary. They died to make it count. These are the ones who have learned the invaluable lessons of hard work because they earned it.

These are our teachers. These are our leaders.

When I ran my first marathon I never imagined how it would change my life. I just ran it because I could. Day after day of training, hard work, dedication, determination, and daring brought me to the starting line in Anchorage, Alaska. And I ran. The paved highway roads, the single-track routes, and the army tank trails through the Chugach Mountain Range. The experience built in me the confidence to do hard things, to set goals, and to do the work necessary to achieve them. I pushed my body beyond what is comfortable, far past the place where I wanted to stop.

I've learned a lot about myself and about dedication, determination, and grit as I have gone on to complete multiple marathons, triathlons, and an Ironman. Through these experiences, among others, I learned that we must boldly design our lives. We must dare to dream and have the courage and dedication to chase those dreams and make them happen.

So often we make excuses for our failures, for rising only to the expectations set before us, or for not even starting in the first place. But the truth is we can do amazing things if we believe in ourselves and, more importantly, believe in something greater than ourselves. It never got easy. It never will. I don't tell you what I have done to brag. It is not to show you what I can do, but to inspire you to what you can do.

Remember where I started? On the sidelines, never an athlete, always a cheerleader. These were seemingly impossible goals for a girl like me. Impossible was made possible, one step at a time. Set a goal, begin, and finish well.

Through thousands of miles and races too numerous to count, I have finished strong—stronger than I ever knew possible, not because I'm special, not because I shattered records or have something you don't. I finished strong simply because I decided to start.

I dug in when the miles got tough and kept on going. Pushing through the grip of pain and exhaustion to the strength that lies in the places we don't even know exist, strength gained from each failure in my past. Each lesson I learned through hardship or trial. Grit formed in the sheer process of determination and dedication. I chose to ignore the whispered lies and fought back with truth. I found personal accomplishment in doing something I never believed I could. Find your race. Find your strong.

So often we get so focused on the road ahead that we forget to look back. The path was hard and the miles were tough, and we're tired and weary and worn from the travel. But it was worth it. It always is because the difficult miles are what have made us. A fighter, a poet, a lover, a friend.

The world will try to break you, the critics defeat you, but your strength is within. Your courage lies in the deepest places when the miles get tough. That is where we draw our strength to stand, where we see we are so much better for the travel.

An athlete may have talent, but it only gets them to good. If they're lucky it might get them to very good. But it'll never take them to great unless they fight for it, unless they give in to the knowledge that our talent is finite and our skill is small, but we serve a God who is big. Wait for great.

MAKING THE COMMITMENT

Where are you? Are you stuck somewhere you don't want to be? *Someone* you don't want to be? Decide. Decide today that you are not going to stay where you are. Our soul knows the depth of our passion and it craves the courage to live it out loud. Have the faith to believe in something for which there is no proof. Our God is faithful and His promises are true.

Take some time to consciously think of where you're headed. Look down the road you are traveling and see where it leads. Is it where you want to go? You have the choice, right now, every day, to bring it back. Course-correct. Redirect. Change!

You may not see yourself there yet. You may not even be able to imagine yourself there, but you'll never get there if you don't set out in that direction. Take a step in the direction you want to go. And then another. Before you know it, you'll look back and be amazed. Step out in faith and let Him thrill you. Let Him fill your empty places. We don't all have to run, but we do need to move. In whatever way you know how, in whatever way God speaks to your soul. MOVE.

Soon you will look back and see how far you've come. You are strong. You are brave. You are doing good work. Keep going. Keep looking back to see. It's a beautiful story, your legacy.

PART FIVE
LOOKING UP

14: PRETTY DEEP
Running to Faith

Faith is being sure of what we hope for
and certain of what we do not see.
~Hebrews 11:1

I often think back to the young woman I was at 21, 22, 23. Those were three very important years of my life, chapters that began the individual faith journey that poured life into the book you hold in your hands. Years, that through failure and brokenness infused the very nature of who I am today. I made decisions and felt rejection and abandonment so piercingly that I could not stay the same. I experienced pain so deeply I literally could not stand.

And so I ran.

It was the beginning of a love affair that was the only solace to my broken heart. There was something healing about being out on the open road, with no one around, and nothing to think about but just breathing. Sometimes it's all we can do. Sometimes it's all we have left.

I would run early in the morning, stumbling out of my house my eyes barely open, the sun barely cresting the horizon. I can close my eyes now and vividly see the trail I would run, when the newly fallen snow cast a blanket of untracked possibility before me, extending an open invitation to make my own path.

It was the start of me living out my faith. And when I say faith I mean it in the true definition of the word: a firm belief in something for which there is no proof.[16] All I had was pieces of a life when my father shared Jeremiah 29:11 with me.

> For I know the plans I have for you, declares the Lord, plans to prosper you and not to harm you, plans to give you hope and a future. Then you will call on me and come and pray to me, and I will listen to you. You will seek me and find me when you seek me with all of your heart. I will be found by you, declares the Lord, and will bring you back from captivity. — Jer. 29:11-14

I was living in a broken down, old football house on a college campus in rural Wisconsin that I couldn't even walk in without shoes. The door didn't lock and the porch was falling off the house. I have no idea what color the carpet was supposed to be. I had to shower in my running clothes and let them air dry in the room I shared with another girl. Disgusting doesn't even begin to describe where I lived for three years. And yet, it is what I had. It was, and is, a part of my story. A lot of healing and great faith took root in those broken down walls.

I taped that verse from Jeremiah to a wall in my room where I could read it every day, several times a day. I remember standing there, fingers touching the words, aching for them to be true, believing that they must because I didn't want to be where I was. I wanted more than anything to be far from where I was.

What tugged at my heart so much about the verse was not only that He knows the plans He has for me to give me a hope and a future, but that I will find Him when I seek Him with *all of my heart*.

I wanted to find Him. I needed to find Him. It was too hard to stand on my own. But I didn't know how, and I certainly didn't have all of my heart anymore. It was broken, and broken badly. But I gave Him my best, and it was enough.

And He has made it anew. It is not the same as it was; it is a new and more beautiful form. He is a God of miracles.

NOT YOUR PARENTS' FAITH

I grew up in a Christian home. We went to church, not every Sunday, but more often than not. I would say there were times growing up when my parents took turns being fanatical and crazy; but, in the end, they both ended up pretty normal, and I'm sure my children will say the same of my husband and I someday. Normal.

If there's anything I've learned so far on this journey of parenting, it is that you can only do your best. Every day, your best. Some days my best is pretty lousy and some days it's okay. Once in awhile it's stellar but, sadly, those days are few and far between. However, every day we have the chance to start again, to change what didn't suit us and try to make the lives of our children better than the lives we had growing up. I believe my parents did that for us, too.

The same is true with our faith. It cannot be our parents' faith. We cannot rest in the faith of our mother or father when we're waist deep in a sinful life. When we're wrestling with heartache, loss, and hopelessness. If we don't have our own faith we'll be tossed by this world.

> Consider it pure joy, my brothers and sisters, whenever you face trials of many kinds, because you know that the testing of your faith produces perseverance. Perseverance must finish its work so that you may be mature and complete, not lacking anything. If any of you lacks wisdom, you should ask God, who gives generously to all without finding fault, and it will be given to you. But when you ask, you must believe and not doubt, because the one who doubts is like a wave of the sea, blown and tossed by the wind.   — James 1:2-6

And what I discovered is that I wasn't ready to find my faith until I had been tossed around a bit—until I lost everything I thought I had.

I've come to believe that much of this life is a process of breaking. That if we desire to truly live, we must first be broken of the things of this world. These earthly shelters, the things and people we cling to for safety, security, and protection. I believe God allows us to come to the edge of breaking, or sometimes to breaking badly, so we can find the end of us because this life is not about us.

As parents, we allow our children to make mistakes to teach them there are consequences, natural disincentives to certain behaviors. How much more does He love us? There is a purpose for each life on this earth and He is looking to use the lives of those who are courageous enough to let the harshness of this world break them, those strong enough to persevere through unknown darkness and hold fast to a faith that would allow Him to rebuild us new. Whole.

So often I try to do life on my own. Worn down by anxiety, fear, insecurity, or worry I believe that if I just try hard enough, work long enough, or do well enough, things will work out for me. How small is my faith.

I was an obedient child. I followed all the rules and lived quite carefully. My parents tell me I never needed a spanking because they only had to look at me crossly and I would cry. It's just how I was made: compliant, tender. But being obedient didn't save me from suffering.

Despite my innate nature, far too often I try to live by my own strength. And God is in the business of breaking us of our idols. For me, it is self—self-protection, self-analysis, self-control, self-reliance, self-centeredness, self-sufficiency, selfishness . . . Self.

Over the last twenty years He's taken me on a journey, stripping me of my own strength and shaking the security I have clung to in this life, providing nothing tangible but the undeserved grace of a redeemer God. His comfort, His love, His faithfulness. His promises.

I truly believe He will use whatever is necessary to bring us to surrender. It is not a question of when, but how. And at what cost? How long will we hold onto stubborn pride before we just let Him do His work in us?

Our faith is grown in the petri dish of a messed up life. Conceived and borne through the desperate places of loss, pain, grief, and unrelenting need. He waits for His children to find their own faith.

GOD ON THE STREET

It was during those years in the old football house where I really encountered God. Not *in* that forsaken house, but during those difficult years. You see, running had become a form of therapy for me—a way to cope with the life I was living and the overwhelming grief of a life I thought was lost.

Most everyone who knows me now sees me as a very fit, active, and independent person. But I wasn't always that way. Up until my mid-twenties I hated being alone. Just the thought made me anxious and insecure.

But life happened. Love happened. Divorce, heartbreak, and rebirth happened.

Quite unintentionally I found my therapy in the silence linked to the rhythm of footfalls on pavement, heartbeat, and breath. A half-mile turned into five, which turned into ten. I remember taking my car to drive the route I had just run. Astonished that I had just run ten miles, I went back to the broken down football house I called home and signed up to run my first marathon (the one in Alaska I mentioned).

It was a goal so beyond my wildest imagining or ability. But it wasn't just a race for which I was training. I was fighting for my life—to pull myself up out of the darkness of a tangled web of loneliness, heartbreak, and failure. I was starting my life over again on my own. Again. I was finding my identity, rebuilding my confidence and my faith.

To me, God isn't in a building. He isn't in a church, a mosque, a temple, or a cathedral. He is in us. He is us. We are the church. And God is in the street.

CHASING OUR TAILS

Some of the most difficult times I've had in my faith are times when I tried to control what was happening. And the truth? The truth is I was afraid that the same story of rejection and abandonment was going to repeat itself. In my mind I thought if I tried hard enough, pled my case well enough, and asked for forgiveness enough, it would be enough. And it never was because I didn't know who I was fighting. I didn't understand what I was up against. There's never a greater enemy than ourselves.

For me, I kept trying to find my mother, whom I loved so very much and yet longed for so much more. I think a subconscious part of me would search for women who were like her, who had similar characteristics to hers, who had the things I wanted to be different in her, and I would try to make them care for me in the way I was missing.

I would try to recreate the story and change the ending, and it failed every time. I cannot recreate my mother; I have a mother. And she loves me in the best way she knows how, with all she can. It has to be enough. Our parents will fail us. Our partners, children, family, and friends will let us down. They will try to be what we need, but ultimately they can never satisfy the desire of our heart. We were made for eternity and we live in a fallen world. Our hearts will never be satisfied here. So often for women, we take that out on our mothers. They're supposed to nurture us; they're supposed to care for us more and better than anyone else. But they're human. Many have their own painful story with their own mother. It's the delicate nature of the mother-daughter relationship—so tender and yet so fierce.

So, who are you searching for? In each of us is a longing to be loved—to be seen and known and valued for the individual gifts and uniqueness we bring to this world. We want to know that our story matters, that the pain and struggle we've crawled through matters. We want to know there is a purpose for our lives and that we matter. We all want the same things, but we search for them in the wrong places. We pursue the wrong methods.

We will never find affirmation on the shoulders of another person. Not our mother, not our father, not our spouse, or anyone else. We can try to throw our needs on someone and they may try to carry it for a while, but ultimately the burden is too heavy. They cannot carry us. They cannot give us what we long for because they haven't even found it for themselves. What we want is our identity, and that is not an earthly assignment. There is only One who can give us what we long for, what we desperately search for in every relationship in this life.

We never know the ending; where this journey of life will take us. But true faith is in the living—tried and tested in the simple things—the daily things. Trust that He will reclaim, redeem, restore, and rebuild every relationship. Every failure. Every misstep, heartache, rejection, sin. He is a God of miracles and He knows who you are. You are His.

ABOUT THE AUTHOR

Tammy Strait is a writer who challenges women to boldly design unhindered lives. She has a Bachelor of Science degree in Psychology with a minor in Communication and graduated from William Mitchell College of Law with a Juris Doctorate. Her passion is helping women live and love with their whole hearts, allowing themselves and others to be free. She and her husband, Kevin, live in Idaho with their three young boys.

CONNECT WITH TAMMY

grace uncommon
BOLDLY DESIGNING AN UNHINDERED LIFE

at www.graceuncommon.com
where you'll find her blog, *Grace Uncommon.*

or on social media at
Facebook.com/graceuncommon
Pinterest.com/tammy_strait

ENDNOTES

1. Codependency, *Merriam-Webster.com*, 2011, http://www.meriamwebster.com (20 November 2013).

2. Darlene Lancer, *Codependency for Dummies,* (Hoboken, NJ, John Wiley & Sons Inc, 2012), 30.

3. Sarcasm, *Merriam-Webster.com*, 2011, http://www.meriamwebster.com (18 December 2013).

4. ABC News Staff, *100 Million Dieters, $20 Billion: The Weight-Loss Industry by the Numbers,* ABC News Staff, May 8, 2012, http://abcnews.go.com/Health/100-million-dieters-20-billion-weight-loss-industry/story?id=16297197

5. CNN, *The Dark Side of Shopping,* Donald W. Black, April 2, 2013. http://www.cnn.com/2013/04/01/opinion/black-shopping-addiction/

6. American Society for Aesthetic Plastic Surgery (ASAPS), Press Center, March 12, 2013, http://www.surgery.org/media/news-releases/cosmetic-procedures-increase-in-2012

7. Ibid.

8. American Academy of Facial Plastic and Reconstructive Surgery (AAFPRS), Patty Mathews, March 2013, http://www.aafprs.org/media/stats_polls/m_stats.html

9. ABC News Staff, *100 Million Dieters, $20 Billion: The Weight-Loss Industry by the Numbers,* ABC News Staff, May 8, 2012, http://abcnews.go.com/Health/100-million-dieters-20-billion-weight-loss-industry/story?id=16297197

10. Anne Lamott, *Bird by Bird,* (New York, Anchor Books, 1994), xxiii.

11. Hinder, *Merriam-Webster.com,* 2011, http://www.meriamwebster.com (10 October 2013).

12. Truth, *Merriam-Webster.com,* 2011, http://www.meriamwebster.com (15 December 2013).

13. Ann Voskamp, *"When All the Negativity and Pessimism is Getting to You",* Ann Voskamp blog post at (in)courage, (May 24, 2013) http://www.incourage.me/2013/05/how-everyone-can-be-an-optimist.html

14. Facebook, *Facebook Statistics,* (January 1, 2014), http://www.statisticbrain.com/facebook-statistics/

15. Elisabeth Sifton, *The Serenity Prayer,* (New York, W.W. Norton & Company, 2003), 277.

16. Faith, *Merriam-Webster.com,* 2011, http://www.meriamwebster.com (3 January 2014).

Made in the USA
Middletown, DE
08 July 2020